MURDER ON YOUNGERS CREEK ROAD

MURDER ON YOUNGERS CREEK ROAD

HOW CAR THIEVES, GAMBLERS, BOOTLEGGERS & BOMBERS IN ONE KENTUCKY TOWN IGNITED A MURDER-FOR-HIRE IN ANOTHER.

GARY P. WEST

Acclaim Press
MORLEY, MISSOURI

Acclaim Press
— Your Next Great Book —

P.O. Box 238
Morley, MO 63767
(573) 472-9800
www.acclaimpress.com

Book & Cover Design: Rodney Atchley

ISBN: 978-1-948901-49-9 | 1-948901-49-8
Library of Congress Control Number: 2019953258

Third Printing 2021
Printed in the United States of America
10 9 8 7 6 5 4 3 2 1

This publication was produced using available information.
The publisher regrets it cannot assume responsibility for errors or omissions.

CONTENTS

Introduction

When author Gary P. West set out to investigate a 1975 murder in the town he grew up in, he discovered it opened a window into a much-larger crime world in Kentucky.

His story extends beyond the horrific murder of an innocent woman to a subculture of underworld contract killers and car thieves in the city he now calls home.

Unlike the Hollywood euphemism "based on a true story," this is a true story.

West's account exposes the sordid past of a southern Kentucky town's more-than-a decade of underworld activities.

Bombings in Bowling Green, Kentucky became old hat ... routine. At the center of it all was whiskey, beer, pinball and slot machines, bookies, bootleggers, and lots of stolen cars.

Before the 1970s, society just seemed to go along with what was put in front of them, a follow-the-herd-mentality. As Vietnam War doubters began to emerge, more people began to ask more questions.

It can be illuminating to expose glimpses into a whirlwind of unlawful activities, and people like to read about it, as long as it's not in "my town." Finally, with a deepening mystery, came a volcanic rush of who and why.

Thank goodness several hard-charging law enforcement officers were about to find out.

Bowling Green, Kentucky, once described by the editor of *Southern Living* magazine as "where the real south begins," sits some thirty miles from the Tennessee border, not far from Nashville. With a major interstate (I-65), highway and parkways skirting the town, Western Kentucky University, an escalation of manufacturing, and the notoriety of being "Home of the Corvette," and the place where Duncan Hines, the cake mix guy was born, it has blossomed into Kentucky's third largest city. Its quality of life has made it appealing not only for business but also for retirees. And it has an economy stable enough to support three private country clubs and three public golf courses.

But it hasn't always been like that.

Throughout the '60s and into the '70s, this southern town, never described as sleepy, earned its reputation as "Little Chicago." Dynamite bombings and bodies being pulled from nearby rivers and creeks were a way of life for some. The largest car theft ring in the United States was organized in Bowling Green. A dragnet produced twenty-two indictments throughout sixteen states that had resulted in over 1,800 stolen cars. As best they could, federal, state, and local law enforcement slowed down this multi-million-dollar, tax-free business.

Some residents weren't sure if law enforcement was doing enough to curb the violence that had enveloped the town. Since most of the bombings, early on, involved liquor and beer outlets and pinball operations, an attitude of "let the bad guys take care of the bad guys" prevailed. That is until a local television tower was blown up. And then when local police itself felt the wrath, things took a different turn.

In Bowling Green, some of the highbrows lived a life of privilege, more concerned about their golf scores, bridge games, and corporate boardrooms, with little or no interest in what was happening in the local poolrooms, beer joints, or nightspots. They paid little attention to stolen cars as long as the cars weren't theirs.

The thought of writing this book had come to writer Gary P. West several years ago. It wasn't an easy decision, and he tells you why.

What makes this story unique is that his family, since the late 1930s, dating back to his grandparents, aunts, and even to his mother, had become the dearest of friends with the family whose son became a key part of a murder-for-hire plot. He found out years later the victim was the mother of someone who had become a very good friend of his professionally.

In other words, he knew the family of the murder-for-hire organizer and the family of the victim.

PREFACE

Some say it was the most notorious murder in the history of Hardin County, Kentucky.

Though it happened in 1975, residents who have lived in and around Elizabethtown, Kentucky, for any length of time still recall it. Time, however, has taken its toll on the facts of this whodunit, once written about in almost every newspaper in Kentucky. It had all the elements. Involving a well-known automobile dealer, two hit men hired to kill him, and a pair of high-profile business partners. It was a story for the ages. The wrong person died, and murder is something that people don't easily forget.

What makes this tragedy unique to me is that I knew the families involved on both sides.

Having spent most of my early years growing up in Elizabethtown and then living sixty-five miles south in Bowling Green for fifty years, it gave me an arm's-length perspective of how the main participants from these two towns came together.

At the same time, I opened doors that I probably shouldn't have but did anyway.

Elizabethtown, often referred to as E-town, is ten miles from Ft. Knox and the famous Gold Vault. Its economy is driven by the military post, one of the nation's largest. Soldiers were in and out on a regular basis, and for car dealers, furniture and appliance stores, and loan sharks, Ft. Knox is a godsend with new business on a rotating basis.

Elizabethtown on the map is called the crossroads of Kentucky and for good reason. I-65, the Bluegrass and Western Kentucky Parkways, and 31-W highway all converge here, forty-five miles south of Louisville.

Scores of people have been interviewed for this book. Many talked freely, some reluctantly, while others not at all.

My aim is to tell the story as factually as possible with absolutely no whitewash.

Like it or not, the public is fascinated with murder. Look no further than movies, TV, magazines, and novels. Why do people kill? How is it accomplished?

One psychologist says that understanding the motivation to murder helps in predicting, preventing, and even protecting against such crimes. As normal people we are intrigued by the motive, the method, and how the killers are caught. We wonder who would be capable of such a crime and whether they are normal like us or hopefully quite different. We can easily be drawn to a real murder because it triggers a basic, powerful emotion—fear.

To tell the whole story required much more than reading old newspaper articles. It was hours spent digging through newspaper files, cranking old microfilm machines until dizzy. Reading hours of trial transcripts retrieved from the National Archives in Atlanta. Time spent in several libraries in Kentucky provided supporting information to countless interviews. I did, however, discover that important tidbits of information can be found by reading obituaries and gingerly walking through a cemetery to find a tombstone.

Fortunately, several very important people involved in the arrest and prosecution of Peggy Rhodes' killers were still around. Their investigative, crime-solving memories rose to the forefront when recounting first the initial report of what appeared to be a terrible accident out on Youngers Creek Road and then the realization it was a murder. Next came the arrest and then the prosecution.

When writing about a murder that happened forty-five years ago, facts can become distorted, memories fade, and a few of those involved are no longer alive. That's why retrieving actual trial transcripts and reading over a thousand pages, not once, but twice, became so vital in getting the facts. But that's only part of the story.

It's easy to sometimes speculate when writing a "whodunit." It's not something a writer wants to do. However, enough circumstantial evidence can and did lead to some speculation.

The product of more than two years of research and interviews and writing, this book details one of the most complex murders and how it brought together two Kentucky towns in an unflattering way.

This story takes a lot of twist and turns that were often like chasing rabbits. And while research can be both frustrating and rewarding, there is much sadness as to how little value is placed on a human life. With little regard to the decades-long impact a crime can have on families of victims, as well as the families of those who commit the crimes, we are left to wonder if the perpetrators realized that dying is forever.

—⁂—

Turning off Hwy. 146 at the edge of town into the Kentucky State Reformatory in LaGrange, Kentucky, a prison located twenty-five miles northeast of Louisville, I quickly realized there are two worlds out there, and my short visit here was just that—a short visit.

I was there to interview a prisoner, Carlos Lloyd.

A couple of months earlier, I had made an Open Records request through the Kentucky Department of Corrections to meet with Lloyd about the book I was writing, *Murder on Youngers Creek Road*. Lloyd knew the title and told me, "I'll tell you the truth, I have nothing to lose."

I've done at least a thousand interviews for books, newspapers, magazines, radio, and television, but never one inside of a prison.

For those who have ever been in a prison, either as an inmate or visitor, you know the drill: empty pockets, take off shoes, raise your hands in the air for a frisk. And I wasn't even flying anywhere.

Once cleared, I went through another set of barred doors into a hallway, where I was met by the prison's public information officer. In the distance I could see a small, grandfatherly-looking man sitting on a bench, leaning forward with his face in both hands. His brown prison garb told me he didn't work here.

Carlos Lloyd and I shook hands, and we were directed into a nearby room, where for the next hour-and-a-half I asked him a series of questions prepared in advance. Sitting directly across from each other, with prison staff looking on, and knowing my time was limited, I got right to the reason I was there. Little small talk, if any, with the only interruption from prison staff occurring when Lloyd, in answering a question, touched on a subject pertaining to an unsolved murder in Bowling Green back in 1971.

The instant Lloyd said Trooper William Barrett's name, the prison official's head popped up from his desk and called the interview to a halt. He called his superiors and then informed Lloyd the Kentucky State Police would be talking to him in the morning. I then continued.

During the interview, a couple of times I had to remind myself that Lloyd was a murderer, a man who had been involved in serious crime most of his life.

Upon leaving, Lloyd and I shook hands again, as I told him I appreciated his willingness to see me. He didn't have to.

"Good luck with the book," he said, catching me a bit off guard. "And good luck to you," I said.

Carlos Calvin Lloyd is scheduled for release in March 2024.

MURDER ON YOUNGERS CREEK ROAD

HOW CAR THIEVES, GAMBLERS, BOOTLEGGERS
& BOMBERS IN ONE KENTUCKY TOWN IGNITED
A MURDER-FOR-HIRE IN ANOTHER.

CHAPTER ONE

"E-town to Unit 796," said a voice over the 100-watt Motorola radio, breaking the silence in the cold, dark night. "Go ahead, E-town," Kentucky State Police trooper Bruce Slack responded.

Darkness comes early in January in Kentucky, and for Trooper Slack it seemed like January 13, 1975, was starting out like just another routine patrol. He was glad that he would have the warmth of his 1974 Ford LTD cruiser to insulate him from the predicted 20-degree, frigid night air.

"We've got a report that a woman has been killed by a horse at her home on Youngers Creek Road," the dispatcher continued.

"I'm on my way," said Slack, knowing that he would have to delay his supper. He was pulling into the parking lot of Jerry's Restaurant on Hwy. 62, not far from State Police Post 4. Hwy. 62 was a straight shot to Youngers Creek Road, maybe six miles. There he would hang a right, drive a couple of miles, cross the overpass above the Bluegrass Parkway, and arrive at the location on his left.

Slack figured he could be there in a matter of minutes. He knew where the house was, even though he didn't know who lived there. And hearing that the lady was already dead as a result of a horse, there was no need to engage his blue lights or put the pedal to the metal. After all, snow had recently covered the roads, and icy patches that remained were difficult to see.

Growing up in LaRue County, adjacent to Hardin County, Trooper Slack knew most of the county like the back of his hand, having often driven by the Youngers Creek Road residence.

Upon turning onto the long driveway, everything seemed normal, no one standing outside waiting for his arrival. A couple of cars with their engine still warm were parked near the house, indicating others had just arrived.

Quickly looking around, he saw nothing in the dark night and walked toward a door that opened into the kitchen, where he was met by Dr. Clyde Brassfield and Paul Gfroerer, the son of the home's owner, Paul "Dusty" Rhodes, a Ford dealer in Elizabethtown.

Dr. Brassfield had received a call some forty-five minutes before, telling him to come quick, that something terrible had happened to Peggy Rhodes, who along with her husband "Dusty" Rhodes, had built their 5,200 square-foot brick dream home on Youngers Creek Road, eight miles outside of Elizabethtown.

Dr. Brassfield was a respected small-town family physician who for several years had treated the Rhodes family for all of their aches and pains, but this night, he had seen something not even he had anticipated when Peggy Rhodes' daughter, Ruth, phoned him to say something bad had happened to her mother.

Peering over his gold-rimmed glasses, the fifty-six-year-old doctor informed Trooper Slack that it looked as if Peggy had been killed by a horse down at the barn, a few hundred feet from her home.

With the doctor remaining in the house to comfort Ruth and Ruth's eleven-year-old daughter Susan, Trooper Slack and Gfroerer headed toward the barn.

With a small 2-cell flashlight that Slack had retrieved from his cruiser—under the circumstances, it was the best light source the two of them had—they made their way over the crunchy, icy ground beneath them toward the barn.

Brassfield had described the barn scene as "gory" in preparing the trooper of six years for the worst. Slack was accustomed to investigating criminal activities and, on occasion, very unpleasant situations. He wasn't sure what to expect.

He and Peggy's stepson entered the barn through the opened sliding door, closest to the Rhodes' house at the opposite end of where the reported horse attack took place, a couple of hours before.

Walking into the barn, Trooper Slack's light honed in on a horse lying on the barn's dirt floor covered in debris of soot and wood particles. Almost immediately the small flashlight he used mostly to direct traffic found its way to a human body near the horse.

At first glance Slack wasn't sure what he was seeing. Looking for evidence of a horse attack, the first thing in the barn he saw was a dead horse. It crossed his mind if the horse killed the lady, who killed the horse? When he asked Gfroerer, "Who killed the horse?" he was speechless.

Now mentally processing what was in front of him, he surveyed as much as he could as quickly as he could. Knowing he was not a crime scene expert, he had been well schooled on the importance of preserving what he was seeing. Instantly, something caught his eye in the dirt. He bent over, his light shining on the object, and picked up a 6-volt battery with a small piece of electrical tape stuck to it. A few feet away lay a toboggan that appeared to be the one Peggy Rhodes had worn on her head when she went to the barn. It was twenty feet from her body.

In a matter of seconds, Trooper Bruce Slack knew this was anything but a horse attack. It was a homicide.

Quickly, he and Gfroerer re-traced their steps, heading back to the house. Slack went to his cruiser's radio. "E-town, Unit 796 here," he spoke into the hand-held mic. "Go ahead Unit 796," the voice came back. "We've got a homicide here on Youngers Creek Road. You need to get a detective out here right away."

The first to arrive was Trooper Glen Dalton, who like Slack was pulling a 4-to-midnight shift and who had planned on meeting Slack earlier for supper at Jerry's Restaurant until the call came in about a horse killing a woman.

It wasn't long before the Dusty and Peggy Rhodes' homeplace was crawling with cop cars, Elizabethtown City Police, Hardin County Sheriff's Department, and more. Kentucky State Police cruisers were now ascending on Youngers Creek Road like never before. With more than a dozen vehicles, including the Hardin County Coroner's ambulance, the once-dark night was now ablaze with blue lights.

Detective Sgt. Steve Spurrier arrived next, so did Detective Lt. Walter Sims who would soon take charge in the investigation to see how Peggy Rhodes had died. Not long after, Captain Durwood Roach, Post 4 Commander, drove in from his home in Radcliff, Kentucky, a few miles north of Elizabethtown, just outside the sprawling Ft. Knox military base. It wasn't long before Detective Sims had stepped on one of the barn's siding boards scattered on the ground and driven a nail through his shoe and into his foot. Needing some medical treatment, he left.

And then Cpt. Roach also stepped on some bomb debris and had to seek medical assistance. The lighting was bad, and the shadows created by everyone's flashlights made it even more difficult to see.

"It was unbelievable," Bruce Slack recalled years later. "Several cruisers pulled down closer to the barn, so we could assess the scene a little better." "But with all of the shadows, it was almost impossible to make out much about what had happened."

Dalton, Slack, and two other state troopers had the responsibility of patrolling all of Hardin County, which is 630 square miles, making it the fourth largest of the state's 120 counties. Their eight-hour shifts seldom ended when they were supposed to. It seemed like there was something going on all the time, and part of being a Kentucky State Trooper was staying with the job until it was done. Forty-hour work weeks looked good on paper but, in reality, rarely happened. And the night of January 13, 1975, into the wee hours of January 14, all hands were on deck to secure a crime scene with very few known facts.

The only thing known for sure was that Peggy Egbert Rhodes, age fifty-seven, and a horse lay dead on the barn floor near her home on Youngers Creek Road.

CHAPTER TWO

When the day had began, Peggy Rhodes thought little about any-thing but doting over her eleven-year-old granddaughter, Su-san, who had spent Sunday night with her and Dusty at their farm on Youngers Creek Road.

Susan had been ill with a fever and upset stomach, so she would spend Monday with her grandmother instead of going to school.

Early that morning, Dusty, who had sold his Ford dealership several months earlier, said goodbye to Peggy and left his 1,200 acre farm a few miles east of Elizabethtown. Now considered a gentleman farmer, he was headed up the Bluegrass Parkway to Frankfort, Kentucky's state capital, to take care of some farm business. Driving his new 1975 ma-roon Thunderbird, the trip would take him little more than an hour. The lightly traveled Parkway was tailor-made for him. He was on friendly terms with most of the cops, and even if he did sometimes have a lead foot, he could drop a few names and be none the worse for it if pulled over. His Ford business serviced all their police cruisers, so he knew most of them by name.

Peggy's daughter, Ruth, lived in Elizabethtown and Peggy's other granddaughter, thirteen-year-old Lara, a sixth grader, headed off to school while her mother went to work at Crucible Steel.

That afternoon Peggy talked on the phone to a couple of friends be-fore calling Ruth at 4 p.m. to give her an update on Susan. She said she had a roast in the oven, and since Ruth would be coming out to pick up Susan, she might as well come for dinner. She knew Dusty would be home, and there would be enough for Ruth and her two daughters. By the way, she said, bring Jerry with you if you want, and we'll play bridge after dinner.

Jerry Gilchrist was a major in the U.S. Army stationed at Ft. Knox and had been dating Ruth Howard, a single mother with two young daughters and a son in the Air Force. He seemed to fit in with Ruth and her family and friends, especially because he liked to play bridge. Peggy told Ruth 5:30 would be fine. That would give Ruth enough time to get home; pick up Lara, her thirteen-year-old daughter; and drive the eight miles to Youngers Creek Road.

The weather, in typical Kentucky fashion, had drastically undergone a drop in temperature. But January was supposed to be cold, and after the first two weeks of the new year that had been unseasonably warm, with one day reaching sixty-four degrees, those warm days went south.

Sunday morning, January 12, the temperature sank to nineteen degrees, a far cry from the high of fifty-four the day before. Monday was no better. With a low of twelve, it rose to twenty-five by mid-afternoon.

As cold weather was setting in, Peggy began to worry about her pets. Buffy, a Siamese cat, never left the house, so that wasn't an issue. She knew Tony, her beloved horse, had the comfort and warmth of the nearby barn, but she couldn't find Binky, her big black cat that looked more like a panther. Binky was more than a barn cat, good only for keeping the mice population down. She often hung out up at the house and over at the oversized pond out front doing what cats do. Peggy thought briefly about the family dogs, Joe-Joe, and Ba-Wa, a blue merle Collie, both of whom hadn't been seen for several days, for some reason.

Oh well, she reasoned, maybe the dogs had ventured off. It was not unusual in rural Kentucky for people to put dogs out on the parkway just to get rid of them, so maybe Joe-Joe and Ba-Wa had taken up with one and gone off for a while. She knew they would eventually show back up when they got hungry. Joe-Joe had been given to Peggy by Jim Johnson, one of the partners who Dusty had recently sold his Ford dealership to.

For now Peggy was worried about Binky. She put on a sweater, a jacket over it, checked to make sure granddaughter Susan was still sleeping comfortably on the couch, and picked up her brown toboggan near the back door. Pulling it down over her ears, she made her way toward the barn

It was 5 p.m. and still daylight when she left the comfort of her home, so she knew she had a few minutes before the sun went down and then it would really be cold and difficult to see.

"Binky, Binky," she called, hoping to quickly get back to the house before Susan woke up and before her roast in the oven overcooked.

Although it was just family coming to supper, she still had a few things to do in preparation for their arrival.

As Peggy slid back the main door to the barn, she was quickly joined by Tony, a chestnut-colored horse with a large swath of white down his face. He was her favorite. On occasion she would ride some of the other horses on the farm, but Tony was the one she enjoyed riding and brushing. This trip to the barn was no different.

Back at the house granddaughter Susan was beginning to stir, waking from her nap. Even at eleven, she felt a little guilty about refusing some medicine her Ga-Ga had tried to get her to take before she nodded off, but now she was wondering where her grandmother was. The only sound she heard was some voices on the TV, and she thought she heard a slamming noise, something loudly hitting something else. But maybe it had come from the television. She wasn't sure. Suddenly the phone rang, disrupting her curiosity about where her grandmother was.

Nina Brandenburg had called for Peggy just to chit-chat about playing some bridge later on in the week.

"I can't find Ga-Ga," Susan told her. "I'm looking for her, and I'll tell her to call you."

Susan opened the back door off the kitchen to the cold late afternoon air. Through the screen, she yelled "Ga-Ga! Ga-Ga!" No answer. Even as a little kid, she reasoned that the only place her grandmother could be was at the barn. She walked bare-footed a few steps toward the barn, and seeing the door was open, she was right in thinking that's where her Ga-Ga was.

Still calling her grandmother's name and getting very cold, she suddenly stopped. Maybe she was imagining it, but she sensed things weren't right. The eleven-year-old's inner self told her to retreat back inside the house.

It was 5:15 p.m., and daughter Ruth had just walked in her home after getting off work when the phone rang at their little house on Crutcher Lane. It was Susan, who hurriedly told her mother she heard a noise like a door slamming and couldn't find Ga-Ga.

Ruth told her she was sure everything was all right but that she would be there as soon as she could. Lara, listening and watching her mother talk to Susan, saw the concern on her face.

Eleven-year-old Susan, seeing the familiar gold recliner that sat in the den in front of the console T.V., curled up in it and waited.

After hanging up the phone, Ruth dialed the number for Jerry Gilchrist in one motion, who quickly came over and picked up her and Lara. For them it seemed as though the drive took forever. They couldn't get to Youngers Creek Road soon enough.

With darkness closing in, Jerry sped up Hwy. 62, not overly concerned about how fast he was going, making a turn, and onto Youngers Creek Road, and then a left into the Rhodes' driveway with the oversized pond on the right. Nothing looked out of the ordinary.

CHAPTER THREE

Susan, now sobbing, all by herself and not knowing where her grandmother had gone, was a scared little girl. She and her grandmother, the night before, had talked about a car that had pulled over and parked up on Youngers Creek Road. It was a bit unusual for cars to stop there, but it was not unusual for cars to stop out on the Bluegrass Parkway. They could easily be seen from the barn and sometime from the house, especially during the winter months when the leaves had fallen.

The traffic count on the Parkway was substantially less than nearby I-65; nevertheless, cars would often pull over near Youngers Creek Road to get under the overpass in a heavy rain or when car troubles popped up.

On occasion, Youngers Creek would flood after a heavy rain, making it nearly impossible to reach the Rhodes' home by car. That didn't prevent Ruth and her daughters from pulling over on the Bluegrass Parkway and hiking their way to the house. It wasn't a difficult walk at all from the Parkway.

On this night, the tires of Jerry Gilchrist's car made crunching sounds on the long driveway to the house, with the barn on the left and the pond on the right. The gravel mixed with the frozen snow was easily heard through the car's floorboard, and all three couldn't help but look out both sides of the windows, hoping to spot Ga-Ga.

Ruth kept asking Jerry, "Where could she be? Why would she leave the house? Do you think she walked down to the pond? Do you think she might have slipped and fell?" Lara, sitting in the backseat, had become upset with the unknowns. She wanted to scream. For her there was a stillness. Something didn't seem right, it felt out of place. Farther down into the horse pasture, looking out of the car's window, those shadows had become menacing to her.

Peggy was nowhere to be seen. Neither was Binky, and neither was Tony. Tony, like many horses, wasn't always kept in the barn, so the horse was usually easy to spot while driving up to the house.

Little Susan had seen the headlights when the car turned into the drive. It was her first bit of relief since waking up from her nap and not being able to find Ga-Ga. She quickly walked from the kitchen into the garage, still in tears.

When Jerry stopped the car, he told Ruth to go check on Susan, and he would look around.

Jerry walked down the slight incline toward the barn. There was a blue glow on the white snow from a nearby security light near the house that didn't quite reach the barn. The only thing Ruth, Lara, and Susan could do was watch Jerry disappear into the darkness, as they stood shivering, listening, and watching in the freezing night air.

Ruth was calling for Jerry. Then she called loudly, "Mother?" That was when their lives would change forever. "Oh my God! Oh my God!" they heard Jerry yell, almost in disbelief.

"Stay where you are," Jerry sternly ordered.

"Where is she?" Ruth demanded. "Have you found her? Mother?"

At first glance, Jerry, in his deep voice, told them it looked like Peggy had been kicked in the head by her horse.

It was so cold that Ruth, now hysterically crying, wanted to get a blanket for her mother and take it down to her at the barn.

"Stay there, Ruth!" Jerry sharply called to her. "She's gone, honey."

Ruth and her two girls slowly made their way back toward the house. No longer thinking about being cold, they were just hanging on to each other. Ruth and Susan were shaking and sobbing, while Lara, who usually kept her emotions bottled up inside, was trying to put all the horrible pieces of what she had heard and seen somewhere in her mind where she could deal with them.

Jerry came through the garage door into the house. Out of breath and visibly shaken from what he had seen, he removed his black-rimmed glasses and wiped his eyes. His face was red from the cold, and with tears frozen to his cheeks, he put his arms around Ruth as she asked why she couldn't see her mother. "I want to see her," she said.

Jerry Gilchrist, a big man with a booming voice, as gently as he could, told Ruth that her mother was dead, and he knew she would not want to see her in this condition.

"Your mother is gone." And then turning the Lara and Susan said, "Your Ga-Ga is gone."

All four were in shock, Jerry from what he had seen, and Ruth and her girls from what they had been told.

Jerry's mind was racing. What had he seen in the barn? Did he see what he thought he saw in those few brief seconds? He was trying to process it all in the minute or less it took him to reach the house from the barn.

Jerry did his best to calm Ruth down. Somehow, she managed to find the phone number to their family doctor Clyde Brassfield, a physician who still made house calls in and around Elizabethtown. At this point in Ruth's hysterical state of mind, the doctor was the first logical person to call. She was still not convinced her mother was dead, and maybe, just maybe, there was something Dr. Brassfield could do. After all, she had just talked to her mother on the phone a couple of hours before. The roast was still in the oven. She couldn't be dead.

Dulcie, Dr. Brassfield's wife, answered Ruth's frantic call. Jerry, hearing Ruth trying to explain that there had been an accident, took the phone and told her to send the doctor as soon as possible. He then told the doctor's wife that Ruth might need a sedative because she was in a state of hysteria.

Dulcie Brassfield said she would locate her husband and get him out to Youngers Creek Road as soon as possible.

Still, Ruth was insistent that Jerry get a blanket and lantern and go to the barn and cover her mother. "It's so cold outside," she told him.

With a lantern in one hand and blanket under his arm, Jerry went back down to the barn. This time he went past the dead horse into a section of the barn he had never been in before. He wasn't sure at all what happened. It was confusing, to the point of him not being sure what he was seeing. Sides of the barn torn up, blood everywhere, the missing top part of the horse's head, the barn's floor covered in icy blood, Jerry could make little sense of any of it. He gently placed the blanket over Peggy Rhodes' mutilated body and retreated toward the house.

Seeing another car pull into the drive near the house, Jerry was hoping it was Dr. Brassfield. And it was. The doctor went into the house and in his country-doctor way calmed Ruth and her two girls down. He assured Ruth he would do everything possible for her mother, so he and Jerry headed to the barn with the lantern. For Jerry it was his third trip, and as of yet, the police had not arrived. But there was a reason for that. Early on it appeared to be a horrible accident. Calling the police was not a priority. After calling Dr. Brassfield, Jerry had called Dusty's son Paul Gfroerer, who lived in Elizabethtown. Perhaps he could help in reaching Dusty, who had gone to Frankfort that morning. They knew there would be only one way he would travel, and that would be via the Bluegrass Parkway. Dr. Brassfield later called the police after arriving at the scene.

It was a little after 8 p.m. when Hardin County coroner Dr. James Stuteville arrived. Usually it would have been up to a doctor to notify the coroner, but Dr. Brassfield, occupied by the confusion and trying to minister to the Rhodes family in the house, had not done so. Trooper Slack had called his dispatcher at Post 4, who called the coroner, telling them they had a body on Youngers Creek Road.

Dr. Stuteville was a retired military doctor who had been in his elected position a little over a year. He didn't know what to expect when he reached the barn with the two ambulance personnel who had arrived minutes before him. Trying to focus on Peggy Rhodes' body, he couldn't help but being distracted by all the debris, splintered planks, shrapnel from what looked like nails. To him it looked like some sort of explosion.

Dr. Stuteville waited until law enforcement had taken pictures of what was now a crime scene before ordering the body removed and taken to Hardin Memorial Hospital. It was here that the coroner quickly filed paperwork for an autopsy.

Dr. William Carney, a local pathologist who worked as a state medical examiner, performed the autopsy before Peggy Rhodes' body was released to the funeral home, Dixon-Atwood and Adkins.

Dr. Stuteville continued his investigation. However, based on the facts available to him, including the autopsy report, he rendered his coroner's verdict, finding "the cause of death as injuries, multiple, extreme, secondary to explosive device, detonated."

The coroner officially ruled Peggy's death as occuring on January 13, 1975, at or about 5 p.m. Dr. Stuteville, however, pronounced her dead at 8:10 p.m. on January 13, when he arrived at the barn on Youngers Creek Road and saw the body.

Chapter Four

Dusty and Peggy Rhodes' home on Youngers Creek Road was now swarming with law enforcement, family, and a few friends.

Whatever contraption or device had taken the life of Peggy Rhodes, in doing so, it had changed the lives of everyone who knew her in an instant, especially husband Dusty, daughter Ruth, and grandkids Lara, Susan, and Mike, who was away in the Air Force. Peggy had provided the loving comfort of a wife, mother, and grandmother, and now they were faced with the reality of living the rest of their days without her.

For the grandkids their happiest times had been at Ga-Ga's on Youngers Creek Road. It was there that they always felt safe. Learning to cook, picking blackberries, riding horses, and just having fun on a farm were special takeaways for all of them.

Word travels fast when something bad happens, and even though the Dusty Rhodes farm was "out in the country," there were ways other than the telephone for people to find out that there had been a terrible accident.

Jack Holman was in the plumbing and heating business in Elizabethtown and had a two-way radio in his office and truck. He heard the police talk back and forth that a lady had died on Youngers Creek Road. Jack and wife Rachel were good friends of the Rhodes family, and they, along with Bob and Phyllis Budde, were the first to arrive. Soon after, friends from the Methodist Church were there. Everyone was in shock, but none more than Dusty, who had been spotted on the Bluegrass Parkway by the Kentucky State Police. He was pulled over, informed there had been an accident at his home, and told to follow them.

Pulling into the driveway, Dusty quickly realized this was bad. What on earth? What was going on? Why all the police cars? Where was Peggy? He was in shock, and fortunately, Dr. Brassfield was still there and gave Dusty a shot to calm him down.

Everyone was crying. What had happened in that barn? Dr. Brassfield and Jerry Gilchrist weren't sure. It looked like maybe Peggy had been killed by her horse, Tony. Kicked in the head. They told Dusty there was no way he needed to go to the barn. This man, with a tough, cowboy-like persona, was now crying out loud. He had lost the love of his life.

Total confusion engulfed the inside of the Rhodes' home on Youngers Creek Road. Family and friends were trying to console each other. Few of them noticed the statuette of a horse's head sitting on top of the console TV.

It wasn't long before the house was full of people. Police were sorting things out in the barn, with Troopers Bruce Slack, Glen Dalton, Sgt. Detective Steve Spurrier, and others making sure nothing was disturbed and keeping an eye out for anything that looked out of the ordinary.

Lead State Police Detectives Walter Sims was asking questions. "What did you hear?" he asked 11-year-old Susan. "What did you see?" She told them of the phone call from Nina Brandenburg. The slamming noise. She was trying to think of anything she could. Finally after several hours and thinking this was the worst night of her young life, Susan went home with Jack and Rachel Holman for the rest of the night.

In the meantime, Lara was coping with the tragedy in her own way, serving hot coffee to those who came in the house to get out of the cold or to those who had heard the news of Peggy's accident. She also heard the talk of a horse kicking her in the head. She wasn't sure what to make of it all.

Ruth's son Mike was called. In the Air Force at Anderson AFB in Guam, he immediately made plans to get to Elizabethtown.

Ruth and Lara stayed at the Rhodes' house that night. Lara hung on to her mother, wanting to comfort her. Even as a young girl, Lara saw how distraught Ruth was.

Dusty's good friend, Jim Simon, who had been his sales manager at Dusty Rhodes Ford, came as soon as he heard the news. So did Simon's business partner Jim Johnson.

Simon and Johnson had purchased the Ford dealership from Dusty about a year earlier and over the years had grown close, not only through the business but also through friendship. Simon had learned the car business from Dusty, and Johnson in years gone by had worked as a part-time "birddog" salesman during off-hours from the Kentucky State Police when he had been a trooper at the Elizabethtown Post.

Jim Simon got down on his knees with Dusty, crying and telling him how sorry he was for his loss. "How could anything like this happen," he asked?

It was like this all night long, into the wee hours of the morning. No one slept. How could they when only a few feet away a woman who was liked by everyone had died?

At fifty-seven, Peggy had involved herself in the small community of Elizabethtown. She had served as president of the local Women's Club, was a member of the Hardin Memorial Hospital Auxiliary, active in the town's Bi-Centennial Commission, and her United Memorial Methodist Church was very important to her. The passion she had for the card game of bridge had spilled over to daughter Ruth, and Peggy and Dusty always tried to find time to get with friends to play.

Troopers Slack and Dalton and Larry Milburn were among several others who kept a close eye on the barn, and the comings and goings of anyone they didn't know. They would cover for each other to go to the house, get a cup of coffee, and get warm. It was bitter cold.

Scheduled to end their shifts at midnight, Slack and Dalton remained a presence at the Rhodes' barn until 2 a.m., when they were relieved. For Slack it would be the last time he was there throughout the investigation.

Although the Kentucky State Police had taken charge of the homicide, the Hardin County Sheriff's Department and Elizabethtown Police were involved with anything they could do in assisting.

Once it was determined that Peggy Rhodes' death was the result of an explosive device, Alcohol, Tobacco, Firearms and Explosives (ATF) was notified.

ATF Special Agents Bill Rockliff and Dick Johnston were working surveillance in Louisville that night when their radio pager went off, telling them to contact the state police in Elizabethtown immediately. It was 7:15 p.m. An hour later they pulled into the driveway at the Rhodes' farm. As they arrived, Peggy's body was being removed by two ambulance attendants. Identifying themselves and quickly getting caught up as to what had happened, the two agents grabbed their flashlights and headed down the icy slope to the barn.

ATF agents Rockliff and Johnston quickly scanned the scene outside the barn before entering. Lead Detective Walter Sims had returned from getting treatment for his injured foot and was there to brief them about what he had learned. The Kentucky State Police had taken pictures of the crime scene before Peggy's body was removed, but what the two ATF agents would be looking for was what type of device could cause such damage.

Agent Rockliff had been assigned as the case agent, as he was considered a specialist when it came to explosives. Although only twenty-nine years old, he knew what he was doing. Detective Sims told the agents he thought TNT was the main element of the device. Rockliff and Johnston weren't sure ... yet.

The next morning gave them more light, but due to the cold, the agents took turns going to their car to get warm after crawling around the icy barn floor.

The crime scene was gruesome. The victim and her horse, according to Rockliff, were essentially shredded by the blast. Clumps of blood and pieces of flesh had already frozen. Literally sifting through the debris, the agents were able to find key elements of the device that caused the explosion.

What kind of bomb was it? Every explosion has a power device. What was this one? How was this bomb constructed?

For two days ATF agents scoured the barn inside and out. It was almost unimaginable what they experienced. One agent said he had trouble eating for several days. But it was their job. That's what they had been trained to do. They also knew when it comes to crime scenes, forensics can be the voice for the dead.

Bill Rockliff met Dusty, Ruth, and her two girls. He asked questions and heard the stories. Why on earth would anyone want to kill Peggy? He heard of not one single enemy. But for Dusty ... that was a different story.

CHAPTER FIVE

Paul Dusty Rhodes had been a car guy in Louisville for several years before opening Dusty Rhodes Ford in 1962, on what was then the outskirts of Elizabethtown. It was the hot place to be if you were selling cars.

Dusty had sold Kaisers and Frazer's before opening East Broadway Motors and selling used cars in Louisville in the '50s. He was positioning himself to get a Ford franchise of his own someday.

In 1954, he met an attractive single lady with one daughter, and forever, his life would be changed. He, too, had been married, but this lady, Peggy Mullins, was different. She had a strong, outgoing personality, and the fact that she attained a certain status as one of Louisville's topflight hairdressers showed Dusty that this lady was successful in her own right.

Peggy's daughter, Ruth, was fifteen years old when her mother decided to go to cosmetology school in 1950, and over the next several years, Peggy's reputation grew as one of Louisville's most well-known downtown hairstylists. She was so much in demand that Alfred Allen, who owned what was considered the city's best-of-the-best hair salons, enticed Peggy to move to his shop on Shelbyville Road in the Plaza Shopping Center.

Ruth, in the meantime, had attended Girls High, which would be blended into Louisville Manual High, where she was part of the first graduating class of boys and girls in 1951.

Dusty and Peggy were married in 1955, and not long after, Peggy left the cosmetology business.

In 1961, Dusty Rhodes finally got his wish. A Ford dealer development franchise became available in Elizabethtown when Taylor Watt Douglas decided to get out of the business. His Douglas Motors was located in the heart of town, like most other automobile dealerships at the time. It was before the days of interstates, and the fact that 31-W, known as Dixie Highway, was the major corridor from the Midwest to Florida meant there was lots of downtown traffic. Often in the '50s and into the '60s, traffic would become gridlocked while making their way around the courthouse circle.

Because of this in the '60s, Elizabethtown began to expand its business perimeter toward Ft. Knox in order to compete more with Louisville. Even though the Army facility housed the Gold Vault, it was the thousands of soldiers and their families stationed there that was the real gold mine. Their steady paychecks were tailor-made for furniture and appliance stores, pawn shops, loan sharks, and a new thing called "fast food."

Before it was Ft. Knox, it was called Camp Knox, and an Elizabethtown entrepreneur named Horace McCullum saw the business potential of always having an inventory of "new customers" because of the continuous turnover of soldiers coming in and out. He bought some land in 1919, subdivided it into thirty-nine building lots, and auctioned them off. He also opened a general store just outside the Army post and then declared the community to be Radcliffe, named after a military friend of his, Major William Radcliffe. Somewhere along the way the "e" was dropped, and it wasn't until 1956 that Radcliff became an official Kentucky city.

As Ft. Knox grew, so did Radcliff, and it was then that Elizabethtown businesses began to work their way in that direction. Car dealers decided to no longer let Louisville have the upper hand, so most of the major brands constructed dealerships with large showrooms and state-of-the-art service departments. After all, what young soldier didn't want to buy a shiny new car?

Paul Rhodes, in 1962, moved to Elizabethtown and opened Dusty Rhodes Ford on 31-W north, on the outside of town. Before long most of the Elizabethtown dealers were there, all within a mile of each other. In fact, it was common for them to run joint advertising campaigns featuring the "Miracle Mile of Auto Sales."

Dusty's nickname came from 1954 New York Giants World Series hero Dusty Rhodes. From then on if your last name was Rhodes, you were called Dusty

Dusty and Peggy quickly became a big part of the Elizabethtown community. Neither were what you might call "high hats," but they, nevertheless, became involved in the community, with Dusty active in the business world and Peggy volunteering in local projects.

Business was good. Dusty was selling lots of cars in spite of there being two other Ford dealerships in the area, Osborne Motors in Radcliff and Knox Motors in Muldraugh, a wide place in the road on the north side of Ft. Knox. Muldraugh's claim to fame perhaps is several scenes of 31-W businesses in the James Bond movie *Goldfinger*.

Not long after, in 1963, Dusty and Peggy decided they wanted to move to the country. Dusty had always wanted to be a farmer, so when he purchased over a thousand acres of land out in the country, just off the Bluegrass Parkway on Youngers Creek Road, he and Peggy soon made plans to build their dream home. Even though their new property butted against the Bluegrass Parkway, there was no exit from the parkway at the time. It came several years later at Exit 8.

Although Peggy had lived in Louisville for several years, she was by no means a city girl. Having been born in Princeton and lived in Lebanon, these two Kentucky communities had helped to develop her small-town values. So, now it looked like Dusty could do his farmer thing, with cattle and pigs, and Peggy could have her horses.

Together, they built a 5,200 square-foot, ranch-style home and a couple of barns, and Dusty had dug out a large pond just off to the right of the long driveway that led to the house.

Life was good, and Peggy enjoyed the visits from Ruth's three children, Mike, Lara, and Susan. She loved being a grandmother. As far as Ruth was concerned, Dusty was her dad, even calling him that. Her natural father had died when she was five, so Dusty had become a big part of her life. The grandkids loved Dusty, too, and called him Dah-Dah.

Cars weren't the only thing Dusty sold at his dealership. He had the Ford Tractor franchise on the same property, which made it easy to oversee both operations.

Dusty was always buying and selling, even owning a 3,500-acre farm in addition to the farm he and Peggy lived on.

Billy Frank Harned, in the early '70s, had worked for Dusty one summer while adding another layer of knowledge on his way to becoming a successful auctioneer in Bardstown, twenty-five miles from Elizabethtown.

Harned got to know Dusty well. In 1974, he purchased 300 acres from him, and over the next several years, the two had maintained a good relationship.

"Dusty was a risk taker," Harned said. "He'd buy things nobody else would want to touch, and he made money on it, too."

One venture Dusty didn't make money on was his pig farming. He needed feed and lots of it. After working out a deal with Ft. Knox to take all the leftovers from their mess halls, he purchased a couple of the big tanker trucks to do the job. Someway, somehow, the contract was cancelled, and Dusty was left with two empty trucks and a bunch of hungry pigs. He lost money.

Some said Dusty wasn't really a farmer, even though he wanted to be. His true talent was selling cars, especially used cars.

Jimmy Lee and his brother had operated Lee's Gulf Service at the corner of Floyd and Breckinridge just down the street from Dusty's car lot in Louisville. When Dusty asked Lee to be his parts and service manager at his Ford dealership in Elizabethtown, he accepted.

"Dusty was a true car salesman," Lee said. "He was free hearted, and if someone was in need of money, he'd give it to them. But when it came to cars, he could wheel and deal. He was the best."

Dusty, it seemed, always had something for sale. It could be his farm, his Ford dealership, or his cattle he sold across several states. A couple of times he was close to selling his car dealership to Hull-Dobbs Ford in Louisville.

Peggy usually drove a Crown Victoria LTD, and on several occasions, Dusty would call her while she was playing bridge somewhere and inform her that he had just sold her car. Someone would come and pick her car up. She would often laugh to her friends that she didn't know from one day to the next what she would be driving.

Dusty's car of choice would be a new Thunderbird. He had a Ford pickup on the farm, but it was his T-bird that he treated like a truck. He was notorious for driving it through fields to check on cattle, and once he even drove it into a sinkhole on his property and called a wrecker to get him out.

It was also no secret that Dusty liked his bourbon, sometime to excess, but for the most part, he kept it under control. It was said the bourbon fit in with his white cowboy hat and the cigar-chomping image he projected. Some of his associates said the art of the deal for Dusty was whatever was in his best interest.

Whenever you sell something, there's always going to be someone who is not happy, especially if you sell cars. An unhappy customer sometimes comes with the territory.

Charlie Wise was a young man in Elizabethtown on the fast track to make some money. He worked for a while selling Ford tractors for Dusty and then invested in his farm operation. Wise was twenty-one at the time and recently married in 1973, when he said he lost $17,000. "I'd work to midnight plowing and setting out crops," Wise recalled. "The money I lost through Dusty was a lot of money back then."

Wise was just one of several who was not happy with dealings they had had with Dusty Rhodes.

It didn't take the Kentucky State Police long to figure out that the explosion that killed Peggy Rhodes wasn't intended for her at all. They were certain that Dusty had been the target.

CHAPTER SIX

I nitially everyone was a suspect in Peggy's death. At the head of the list was Dusty. The spouse is always questioned, no matter how perfect a marriage may seem. Investigators quickly cleared him. Anyone who knew the couple knew he loved her unconditionally and she did him.

Everyone in and around Elizabethtown was talking about Peggy's death. It wasn't clear if someone was trying to kill her or even another person. Perhaps it was just a scare tactic.

In a state police news conference one week after the explosion, Detective Lt. Walter Sims offered that the bomb was military-type compressed TNT and that laboratory analysis of the evidence collected at the scene was 99 percent sure the explosion was caused by the non-commercial compressed TNT and a commercial-type blasting cap.

"That rules out dynamite," Lt. Sims said. "We never did smell any dynamite. And it rules out any fire explosives. There wasn't a fire."

He went on to say the explosive device was "pretty sophisticated" and had to be assembled by someone who knew what he was doing. It was not the type of device that could be set up by the average layman, Lt. Sims said.

The average person might say, "What difference does it make whether it was TNT or dynamite?" For this murder, it was very important.

TNT (trinitrotoluene) is an explosive used in military shells, bombs, and grenades, as well as for industrial uses and underwater blasting. TNT production in the United States takes place only at military arsenals. It is a chemical compound.

Dynamite, on the other hand, is a stabilized form of nitroglycerin and more powerful than TNT. Alfred Nobel, of Nobel Peace Prize fame, invented dynamite in 1867 for the purpose of revolutionizing the process of construction, demolition, and mining. But then others saw another use for it—killing people.

The bomb had been rigged to the tack room door, which was a storage area for some of the horses' gear. It was next to the feed room. Inside the tack room were a pair of permanent wooden ladders leading to the barn's loft where hay was sometimes but not always kept.

Lt. Sims' comments led investigators to begin looking toward Ft. Knox. With the military-type TNT and fragments from a metal container, perhaps an ammo box, being found, it was natural deduction. This could have been what housed the putty or granular blocks of TNT weighing anywhere from one-quarter pound to one pound.

The way the explosive device had been described led some to believe it was a booby-trap set-up, with trip wire that, when touched or moved, exploded. It sounded like something that had been used by and against U.S. soldiers in Vietnam. There were probably several at Ft. Knox who had experience with such a device.

Over the years Dusty had had a few dissatisfied customers who had been in the military. He had sold hundreds and hundreds of cars and trucks to soldiers, so investigators searched out those who might be obvious suspects.

With Lt. Det. Sims leading the probe for the state police, Special Agent Frank Guernsey reported that several ATF agents were involved in the investigation. Their presence was a result of a crime committed with a destructive explosive device.

It seemed like everyone in Hardin County had an opinion about the Youngers Creek Road murder. Lots of questions, too. Why weren't the dogs barking that night or the night before? "Peggy was always playing with her dogs," said Kenneth Peeples, who lived across the road from the Rhodes' farm. But for some strange reason, the dogs had disappeared. With granddaughter Susan asleep on the couch, Peeples may have been the last person to see Peggy alive when he saw her jogging to the mailbox and back, like she always did around 3 p.m. that Monday afternoon on January 13, 1975.

Lt. Sims said the Rhodes murder was the major investigation for Post 4. "We are devoting 90 per cent of our time to the case," he said.

Hardin County was not accustomed to homicides. In 1974, there had been three. In 1975, Peggy Rhodes' death was the first of five.

Polygraphs, thirty-five of them, were taking much of the time, as investigators were talking to anyone they could find who had had financial dealings with Dusty.

One of those who went to Post 4 was Charlie Wise.

"They asked me if I smoked ... I said no," recalled Wise. "I didn't, but it (the needle) went off the chart because I had indeed smoked before. They told me that day I had nothing to worry about, and I didn't."

It just so happened that by mid-February, the Kentucky State Police were also investigating the January 4 robbery and shooting of Jack Cranmer, manager of Happy Hollow Farm near Colesburg, not all that far from the Rhodes' farm.

Cranmer said a man knocked on his door at 3 a.m. and asked him for help pulling his car out of a ditch on a nearby road. After Cranmer had pulled the car out with his tractor, two other men came out of the car and beat and robbed him. The man who had asked for help shot Cranmer at close range with a .22 caliber pistol after saying, "Don't leave no evidence." The three got $39, and Cranmer spent two weeks in the hospital.

Could these three cold-blooded robbers with intent to kill have had anything to do with the Rhodes murder nine days later? Were they casing the area?

By late afternoon on January 14, most of the crime scene investigation had been completed. Lt. Sims had not physically participated in the investigation but was charged with coordinating between Kentucky State Police and the ATF. Admitting that he was "not well experienced" in investigating scenes where explosives had occurred, Lt. Sims said, "We don't have too many explosives around here."

Through all the early investigation by the state police, no written reports were submitted. It was all verbal.

In a short time, the investigation was turned over to State Police Laboratory Technician Ronald Freels out of Frankfort.

Special Agents Rockliff and Johnston had joined Freels in physically crawling on the barn's floor, sifting through the smallest of particles to recover pieces of evidence.

A leg wire, which is a wire running from a board, was found. So were pieces of a board with a contact mechanism, tape, and some nylon string wrapped around the mechanism. Latent fingerprints were also discovered.

Rockliff was trained in bomb scene searches, part of which is to look for physical evidence that could tell him what destructive device was used. Wrappers used around dynamite was one of those items he was trained to look for. He knew that dynamite comes in various configurations and sizes, usually in wrappers.

Agents Rockliff and Johnston found no wrappers. Their absence didn't necessarily mean dynamite was not used but instead meant if dynamite was used, the wrappers had been destroyed or removed before the bomb was constructed. Wrappers were important because they normally had codes and numbers printed on them, revealing their origin.

State Police Technician Freels turned over the evidence he had to Agent Rockliff, who personally drove it to the Bureau of ATF Laboratory in Cincinnati for a more sophisticated analysis to isolate exactly what had caused the explosion.

(Two years later in 1977, Freels was involved in the investigation of the Beverly Hills Supper Club fire that claimed 169 lives. He had, according to Robert D. Webster's book *The Beverly Hills Supper Club*, taken hundreds of color slides and photos and not turned them over to the state police, retaining them for his own personal files.)

It's not unheard of, but it is somewhat unusual when a reporter covering a story becomes part of the story.

Ron Kapfhammer was proof that you don't have to work for a big-city newspaper to be good. He doggedly stayed with the Rhodes murder. After all, it was the biggest murder in the area in years, and he knew the newspaper's readers were clamoring for more in this whodunit.

Kapfhammer, in the *Elizabethtown News-Enterprise*, reported that Lt. Sims had ruled out dynamite, saying he was 99 percent sure it was military-compressed TNT. Even though Sims stated state police had done an analysis, they hadn't. It was over two months later that the analysis came back. It was not TNT.

It was never brought out that Kapfhammer's mother, Dorothy, worked as a dispatcher for the Elizabethtown City Police Department. Though the department wasn't involved in the investigation, a dispatcher would be in a position to hear all of the "noise" between the state police, the sheriff's department, and the ATF. And what mother wouldn't want to help her son?

Gerald Lush was the editor of the *News-Enterprise* in 1975. "We had a couple of threatening phone calls back then about our coverage of the case," he remembered. "I picked up the phone, and the caller said I'd better back down on my coverage of the case or he would come over and blow my f-ing head off." Shortly after, Ron Kapfhammer came running into my office saying he'd gotten a call from someone telling him to quit writing about it or he was going to get killed.

"Ron said he'd called the state police. They told him they couldn't do anything until something happened. Ron told them by then it would be too late."

With pieces of the murder puzzle beginning to fit, the depth of the investigation was far more intense than most Hardin County citizens realized. Many of the leads led family and law enforcement down dead ends. Every lead, regardless of how outlandish it seemed, was looked into. The perpetual tension and anxiety were taking their toll as daily rumors took on a life of their own.

The TNT-versus-dynamite debate was a key factor in that there had been a bombing in Bowling Green, Kentucky, sixty-five miles south, the year before with some similarities. With Lt. Sim's assertion that it was TNT in the Rhodes bombing, it could rule out a connection. Dynamite, on the other hand, would be a connection.

James Young, an explosives expert, offered that there is a property common to Hercules dynamite that's not found in any other dynamite. It was course-ground walnut hulls that were used as a filler material.

Young added that the bomb that killed Peggy Rhodes was commercial dynamite. Not military. Not TNT. He was certain. Considered an expert in the components of explosives, he had testified in twenty trials.

The laboratory in Cincinnati maintains a reference file of known manufacturers of leg wires made in the United States, and the leg wires found in the Rhodes' barn were compared to the ones the ATF lab had on hand. And it was Hercules that used the same color and size wire.

Everyone was still asking why Peggy? Sometimes "hits" had been put on family members as a way of showing someone else in the family they were not safe … or maybe were next.

Every other day, a farmhand had come to the Rhodes' farm to feed their cattle and the horse in the barn. He had been there Sunday morning before the late Monday afternoon explosion. He said he had been in the tack room and in the barn's loft, where hay is stored. Or could it have been the feed room and not the tack room?

The night Peggy Rhodes mangled body was brought by ambulance to the morgue at Hardin Memorial Hospital, former Hardin County

Sheriff and U.S. Marshal Charlie Logsdon was there by happen chance with his gravely ill wife. Logsdon couldn't help but notice the commotion and asked what had happened. When informed, he told several people, "If it's dynamite, you need to look toward Bowling Green. Down there, they blow up everything."

Bowling Green? But why would anyone there want to kill Peggy Rhodes?

Bowling Green didn't have the market cornered on violence. In fact, it was not quite at the level of what had been going on in Northern Kentucky, particularly in Newport. While Bowling Green was known as Little Chicago, Newport had the distinction of being called Sin City.

Newport was pretty much run by the Cleveland Mob, and as far back as 1940, the area had some forty-five illegal gambling casinos. The town was consumed with gambling, murders, and prostitution.

CHAPTER SEVEN

O n May 24,1974, a mobile home sales office was bombed in Bowling Green, sixty-five miles south of Elizabethtown.

In the 1950s throughout the 1960s and into the 1970s, Bowling Green was considered a regional area for shopping, entertainment, and medical care. With a major highway thoroughfare known as Dixie Highway passing through the middle of it, and later I-65, the town was on the brink of an economic explosion. But that wasn't the only thing exploding across Bowling Green and Warren County.

Crime, by way of gambling, car thefts, bootlegging, and illicit liquor and beer sales, had engulfed enough of the local underworld that the county judge offered, "We'll see a reduction in the type of criminal activities when most of the bad guys are killed off by the other bad guys."

Not necessarily a ringing endorsement to make the rest of the county feel safe, but local law and order was there to take care of that.

Or were they?

Rumors abounded as to just how passionate Bowling Green's finest were about the job they were hired to do.

With low pay that often leads to low morale, here was a police force that numbered anywhere from thirty in the '50s to fifty-five in the '70s. Many of the officers took on second jobs during their off-duty time.

However, a few incorporated their second source of income into their on-duty time while cruising Bowling Green, especially at night.

One former Bowling Green policeman said it was common knowledge among the force that several of his fellow officers were up to no good. "They would take orders for tires and, at night, visit tire stores who had left their inventory or displays out, get the tires, and load them in the trunk of their patrol car. Another officer had rigged up a coat hanger apparatus, where he could reach into a night deposit box and pull out some of the deposit bags. Who's going to question a cop car late at night at a bank? Back then most night deposits were cash and checks. Credit cards weren't in wide use at the time."

Even though the murder of Peggy Rhodes had occurred in 1975, it's interesting to look back and see how Bowling Green culture had emerged as a crime-laden little city that its own citizens referred to as "Little Chicago" and not because of the wind. To understand the depth of the murder on Youngers Creek Road, it would be an injustice not to look at the criminal climate in Bowling Green, which eventually became intertwined with Elizabethtown.

Bernie Cox joined the force in 1970, after being a part of the nearby Russellville Police since 1966. So, he was well aware of all the activity going on in both Warren County and Logan County.

"Lots of activity back then in downtown Bowling Green," Cox said. "All of the bars, entertainment, restaurants, and shopping was all downtown."

Police cars in those days had no air conditioning, and it was a common practice in the '60s and '70s for off-duty officers to ride around with those on-duty, just to keep them company during their shift.

Poker, craps, and horses were easy findings in Bowling Green, especially when it came to John L. Edwards. Articles were written about him and his prowess with the cue stick. "With Johnny you could get a lot of bets on just about anything at his pool room downtown," said a Bowling Green lawyer. "But you'd better know what you were doing if you were shooting pool."

John got his gambling genes from his father John L. Edwards Sr. who as far back as the early 30s operated a little roadhouse on Beech Bend Road. He was said at the time to be the largest bookie in Kentucky. So successful was Edwards Sr. that when he built the house, it was built around his safe.

He passed that knowledge onto John Jr., and despite thick Coke-bottle glasses, John Jr. was a world-class pool shark. Supposedly, Minnesota Fats told an Edwards family member that Bowling Green had more action than anywhere in the country when it came to booze, money, and gambling. Fats was also fascinated with a particular nightspot in town. Lost River Cave's underground nightclub was something he said he'd never seen anything else like in the world.

There was another vice that had become a fixture in Bowling Green, and for over thirty-five years, regardless of the state of politics, little was done about Pauline's on Clay Street.

Any "planned" raids on her establishment were preceded by tips she received, and whenever the Warren County Grand Jury was in session, Pauline's would be closed for "vacation or remodeling."

Pauline Tabor first opened her brothel on Smallhouse Road in 1933, before finally moving it to what would become her famous location on Clay Street in mid-1940. There wasn't a soldier at Ft. Knox or Ft. Campbell or a student at nearby Western Kentucky University who didn't know the address. It did, however, take the government to close her and her girls down, when in 1968 her house was lost to an urban renewal development. The famous Pauline went on to write a book that made many of the locals very nervous. She even appeared on national talk television shows with Dick Cavett and Johnny Carson.

In 1957, an organization called the Anti-Alcohol Association in Warren County implemented a successful drive to get a local option "wet-dry" vote on the ballot for a special election on September 17, 1957. The county had permitted liquor sales dating back to the end of Prohibition in 1933. By an almost two-to-one vote the anti-liquor forces prevailed by a margin of 4,712 to 2,863.

The result soon brought about a proliferation of bootleggers, and by 1960, the *Bowling Green Daily News* reported Police Chief Horace Snell as saying, "The bootlegging situation in Bowling Green is out of hand, despite diligent efforts of law enforcement officers."

Two-and-a-half years of no legal liquor had worked well for some. But for others, not so good.

Records revealed some 200 arrests tied to bootlegging in the several months following the vote taken in 1957.

With something needing to quickly be done, the local powers that be were able to get another local option special election. But this time it was city-only. Many thought this would have a direct impact on the bootlegging trade and let normal life return to Bowling Green in Warren County.

The city-only measure passed by a huge margin, 6,670 to 3,920, leaving Bowling Green as an alcohol oasis for all the thirsty surrounding dry counties.

Whenever someone is getting into their pocketbook, it usually doesn't end well.

And in the case of bootleggers, the retaliation of choice was dynamite.

Many of the bombings were attributed to disgruntled bootleggers ending the dry period. Bowling Green liquor dealers and wholesale beer distributors offered a $1,000 reward for solving the bombings. As many of the criminal tentacles reached out, some were even shaking down liquor stores for protection against being bombed.

In no time, a turf war developed among bar and liquor store owners, some of whom would go to any means to protect their territory, even if it meant murder.

Cars and trucks would be seen leaving Bowling Green for another county, and according to a former Bowling Green police officer Jim Rogers, in a *Bowling Green Daily News story* said, "They would be so loaded down with half pints they'd almost burst their springs."

Rogers went on to say, "A lot of places would have delivery services. The buyers wanted a scheduled delivery at 4 a.m. before the local sheriff woke up."

The local leaders of the criminal element used violence to eliminate competitors, snitches, or lawmen to send a "back-off" message. And dynamite was the choice of weapon. It was easily obtained from rock quarries or farms and the results left little evidence.

As it turned out it wasn't just liquor that contributed to the apparent lawlessness. Liquor stores and bars were also trafficking in stolen merchandise, pinball machine gambling, slot machines, and food stamp fraud.

Vending machine companies also competed against each other, and there were several in Bowling Green that serviced legal and illegal venues throughout surrounding counties. It wasn't just the pinball machines they delivered and serviced but also jukeboxes, cigarette machines, and coin-operated pool tables.

"When we lost a customer, it was usually because another vendor had a newer model than we did," said a former vendor who operated in the '60s and into the '70s.

"We always tried to stay on the good side of Papa John (Bryant) and his son Jimmy," he said.

It was the Bryant's who were recognized as the area "kingpins" of beer, liquor, and lots of other activities in southcentral Kentucky during that period. Jimmy Travelsted was another Bowling Green local who did lots of liquor and beer business in surrounding counties.

Bowling Green civic clubs were pleading for the public and police to do something to at least slow the crime wave down, if not stop it. The bombings and attempted bombings had resulted in a huge monetary loss. The local Rotary Club in a statement said, "The degradation of our community in the eyes of it's citizens, and the people of this state and nation, is even a greater loss."

In September 1961, Warren Circuit Judge John B. Rodes demanded a grand jury to make investigating the bombings a priority. The city commission even put up a $2,000 reward for information.

"We are a city of 30,000, a city of homes, a city of churches, a city of schools—that's our strength," Judge Rodes told the grand jury. "We aren't going to permit any lawless land to destroy all this."

It wasn't that Judge Rodes' words fell on deaf ears, but it was simply that the violence continued.

In one year in the mid-'60s, the *Daily News* reported that Warren County had thirty-two homicides, a murder rate seven times higher than the national average. In the '60s, Warren County population figures showed 45,000, whereas, in recent years the county typically showed fewer than ten homicides a year. In 2019, Bowling Green, with a population of 62,000, recorded only four homicides.

Anytime you have gambling, liquor, and beer as key components of a lifestyle, there's a good chance the end result will not be good.

History shows that criminals often steal from each other, cheat each other, and even kill each other. And around Bowling Green throughout the 1950s, John Noah Johnson, who went by Buster Johnson, had established his own piece of the local underworld, staying just out of reach of the law.

Buster Johnson, according to his son Don, was a big-time hustler, anything to make a buck. That meant dealing in slot machines and pinball machines, fencing cigarettes, gambling, and selling liquor and beer.

Johnson owned a 200-acre farm at Flat Rock in the northern part of Warren County. An oversized garage was used to store liquor and beer that would later be delivered to "dry" clubs and poolrooms around Bowling Green.

"My dad had so many people on his payroll that included several policemen," said the younger Johnson. "He was always on the lookout, but he was pretty much left alone. This was a big operation."

"Dad bought Fall City beer out of Louisville and two truckloads of just beer would be delivered to us at Flat Rock twice a week. I helped load the conveyor belt when those trucks came in. I'm a little kid just doing what I was told.

"Dad was able to get in most of the big truck stops. They were very lucrative," Don Johnson continued. "But those truck stops wanted up-front money to locate there. American Legion and V.F.W. clubs were also great places for slots."

Buster Johnson had three full-time route collectors.

"I was twelve when I started running routes, collecting for slots, jukeboxes, and cigarette machines," Don said.

In 1959, the elder Johnson rented a warehouse on College Street in Bowling Green, where he kept the amusement equipment. The liquor and beer, however, remained at his Flat Rock farm.

Don Johnson says that anything anybody stole back then they brought it to his dad. But perhaps Buster's largest fencing operation took place when he bought a tractor trailer full of cigarettes stolen from Brown-Williamson in Louisville.

"He stored them at Flat Rock and College Street because there were so many of them," Johnson said. "It took him a year-and-a-half to completely fence them."

In 1960, Bowling Green citizens voted to go wet once again, and Buster Johnson's liquor business came to a slow halt. It wasn't long after, in 1963, that newly elected Gov. Ned Breathitt declared all slot machines illegal in Kentucky.

"The state picked all of them up, even with money still in them," Don Johnson recalled. "Locally they stored them in the old downtown Armory. Dad hired attorney Ernest Gregory to help recover them, but he was unsuccessful."

Anything dealing with gambling devices seemed to be off-limits for Gov. A.B. "Happy" Chandler (1955–59), and Gov. Bert Combs (1959–63). They were reluctant to interfere in what both termed to be local matters.

Gov. Breathitt, however, felt like Kentucky's gambling had begun to take its toll on the quality of life in the state. It was a little-known fact that he considered pinball machines at the head of the list of gambling devices, and he pondered the idea of outlawing pinball machines across the entire state. A murder-for-hire attempt on his life failed. It was thought a major pinball manufacturer was behind it.

Don Johnson went to Western Kentucky University in the daytime, but he had several part-time jobs. One of those was at Park City Mobile Home Sales. It was here that he heard discussion about cars and trucks—stolen cars and trucks.

Dusty and Peggy Rhodes

Peggy riding her favorite horse, Tony, alongside Dusty.

Peggy (GaGa) Rhodes by the lake, her Youngers Creek Road home, with dog Joe-Joe, a gift from Jim Johnson.

Mike in his US Air Force uniform with mother Ruth.

Susan, Ruth and Lara, September 1975.

Rhodes family photo in happier times.

Dusty Rhodes Ford Dealership on 31-W in Elizabethtown.

Dusty Rhodes and parts manager, Jimmy Lee.

Dusty behind desk.

Dusty Rhodes (left) and car dealer Bill Swope playfully point guns at each other for an advertisement.

Advertisement for Dusty Rhodes Ford

Dusty Rhodes standing next to his prized Thunderbird.

Dusty standing outside of his dealership.

Barn crime scene

Investigators look at the crime scene.

Crime scene with dead horse, Tony

Dead horse, Tony

Crime scene

Some remains of the bomb.

Bomb material found in the barn.

Crime scene

Crime scene

Crime scene

Crime scene

Crime scene

Part of the bomb rigging.

Trooper Bruce Slack, first to arrive on the crime scene.

Trooper Walter Sims

Ruth with Jerry Gilchrist

Ruth and Jerry Gilchrist

Ruth, Lara and Susan

Bombing at Park City Mobile Home Sales Office in Bowling Green, 1974.

"When we were young, we drove cars I later found out had been stolen that my dad bought," he said. "If I drove a car I knew was stolen and the heat was on, I'd get rid of it."

As corrupt as Buster Johnson seemed to be in breaking the law, his family saw a lot of good things he did in helping people in need. By the 1970s he had been eased out of the business with his life still intact.

"My dad might have been a gangster or mobster," said Don Johnson, "but he was a very caring person."

Newspapers across Kentucky, Tennessee, and Ohio reported on the dynamite bombings in Bowling Green that revolved around bootlegging, pinball machines, liquor and beer sales, and gambling.

There was a madness to it all, as dynamite bombings were not isolated cases but instead had become routine.

On October 15, 1960, Bowling Green City Councilman and full-time liquor salesman George Dillard had his car blown up. Four hours later Siddens Music Company was bombed. Jukebox and pinball business owner William Siddens had a narrow escape from the five-stick dynamite charge.

Minutes after the Siddens blast, Billy H. Graham, thirty-one, was arrested and held on $10,000 bond.

Graham, however, never went to trial. After making bond, his body was found in nearby Trammel Creek. He had been badly beaten, shot in the head, and an eighty-pound grindstone had been used to sink his body.

The *Louisville Courier-Journal* reported that Selva Wright, fifty-two, and his son, Bobby Wright, twenty-eight, were arrested and each held on $25,000 bond for Graham's murder. The newspaper went on to say the $25,000 bond was the highest in memory in Warren County and that many in the judicial arena of Bowling Green and Warren County felt as though the bootlegging interest had tried to take over.

Another expected witness in that case, Everett Hardcastle, age twenty-nine, failed to appear at a hearing, leading Commonwealth Attorney Morris Lowe to say, "He left town for his own safekeeping." Hardcastle and the Wrights were cousins, and with no witness, the charges were dropped.

The Caribbean Club on east 2nd Street was bombed on January 23, 1961, and less than a month later on February 15, the owners of Cline's First and Last Chance Liquors discovered twenty-nine sticks of unexploded dynamite.

In May 1961, *The Nashville Tennessean* reported that the 31-W Lunch Room, a bar on College Street, had been dynamited on April 28. Rumors of a fight over pinball machine locations and a beer price war were behind it all, the article said. Commonwealth Attorney Lowe pointed out that, "An explosion doesn't leave much in the way of evidence."

A month later on May 27, 1961, the Horseshoe Beer Depot was hit minutes after manager Jerry Gaines had closed for the night.

On August 4, 1961, the *Courier-Journal* wrote that the third bombing in little more than three months happened at Toby's Place on Main Street in downtown Bowling Green. It was the seventh dynamiting in ten months, and two additional bombs had failed to explode, the newspaper reported.

Bowling Green Police Chief Horace Snell said, "No motive had been established and no firm clues were found." He went on to say a sign advertising beer at 15¢ between 4 p.m. and 6 p.m. had just been placed in the bar's window the day before. At that time, other Bowling Green beer outlets were selling drafts at 20¢ and 30¢ for premium. Chief Snell said Toby's Place was holding the line in bottled beer. Three days later, on August 7, the ninth dynamite bomb in nine months was found under the car of Calvin Starks. The five-stick bomb's fuse had burned some fifteen feet before going out. Starks was a part-time worker at the 31-W Lunch Room that had been dynamited the previous April.

Two years later on August 29, 1963, a bomb was found under the car of Bowling Green Police Chief Wayne Constant. It did not explode.

A year later on August 7, 1964, Bowling Green Police Detective Harry Ashby found an unexploded bomb under his car.

Though it might have been unrelated to the Bowling Green explosions, on September 3, 1964, dynamite blasted two office-scale houses of the McClellan Stone Company. One was located in Warren County near Smiths Grove and the other in Edmonson County, just outside of Park City. State police said, "The bombers knew what they were doing, and it looked like three-fourths of a case was used."

Four cases had been stolen from McClellan Stone and were found in a farmhouse thirty-five miles north of Bowling Green. Some of the dynamite found was the same type and identity used in the bombing of the 31-W Lunch Room back in April and the Horseshoe Beer Depot in May.

It was common for rock and stone companies to report thefts of dynamite from their warehouses over the years.

On September 30, 1964, Bowling Green Police Chief Constant's lakeside cabin in nearby Edmonson County was destroyed, not by a bomb but by fire.

"A dynamite bombing is one of the hardest crimes to solve," said Christy Watts, Warren County's Sheriff who came into office in 1965. "Bombings and fires are the two worst kinds of cases because the evidence is destroyed. People are reluctant to come forward because they might become targets."

A late Sunday night dynamite blast on October 22,1967, ripped out the wall of Cardinal Billiards. No one was in the building at the time, which was located just down the hill from Western Kentucky University off College Street and a half-block from Bowling Green High School, where the explosion broke fifty windows out of the school's gymnasium. Once again things were ramping up.

The *Bowling Green Daily News* reported that the Cardinal Billiards owner, Samuel Workins, told police, without elaborating, that he had "been expecting trouble at his place for several weeks."

Police Chief Constant told the newspaper he had talked to Workins about possible trouble, and for three weeks, police had been keeping an eye on the billiards parlor. He said the dynamiting at Cardinal Billiards could not be connected with the wave of dynamiting in Bowling Green in 1960–61 and again in 1964. Earlier in the year, the parlor had been sprayed with rifle bullets after closing hours.

How could the police chief possibly have known this? Did he know something others didn't?

Chapter Eight

Willis Alford was known in and around Bowling Green as a "tough." The former Bowling Green City policeman had walked a tight rope when it came to upholding the law or breaking it. His reputation was that of "if you wanted someone taken care of or a problem solved, he was your man."

In 1956, after being involved in a brawl, it was decided he should resign from the city police force. It was then that Alford became more of a problem than a problem solver for the law.

Because Alford was known to associate with the local criminal elements, some said he carried out some of the town's bombings in the '60s. Other labeled him as a "protector" or "enforcer" for some of those operating in gambling and the liquor and beer wars.

In June 1964, Alford and a former Warren County Constable, Francis Wilson, had been arrested for storehouse breaking in Gamaliel, Kentucky, a small town in Monroe County, several miles from Bowling Green. Wilson had been convicted, and Alford was awaiting trail and out on bond.

On November 10, 1964, police saw a car running a stop sign and traveling at a high rate of speed on the outskirts of town. A pursuit was soon underway, and with speeds reported reaching 100 mph, patrolman L. J. Young radioed for help. Once the car was stopped, police realized the driver was Willis Alford. By now other law enforcement had arrived and positioned themselves to arrest Alford.

According to the official report, as Officer Young approached Alford's car, Alford jumped out, "carrying something that looked like a gun." The report went on to say Alford yelled, "you - - -. I'll kill you." All four officers—L. J. Young, Fred Lancaster, Jerry Hills, and Paul Ramsey—opened fire, killing Alford.

An inquest was demanded by the Alford family, who hired prominent Bowling Green attorney Paul Huddleston (brother of U.S.

Senator Dee Huddleston) who testified almost two hours before a grand jury.

Coroner J. C. Kirby testified that Alford had been shot eight times.

Several officers testified, including Bowling Green Police Chief Wayne Constant and State Police Sgt. Roy Ragland. Circuit Judge Robert Coleman took it a step further and asked them to look into a series of dynamiting in the area.

Two weeks later the grand jury reported: "Acting in the line of duty and apparent self defense is what the police were doing." The grand jury also did not spell out the rumors of alleged payoffs being made to law enforcement officers. They also reported they had devoted five full days to a full investigation.

Still, not everyone was satisfied with how Alford died. Many thought he was set up. And although there were those who knew the thirty-seven-year-old Alford was a dangerous man, they still questioned how he was taken down. And the object in Alford's hand that looked like a gun was said to have been a claw-like garden tool.

Probably not connected to other area explosions, on October 2, 1968, a blast occurred at Cutler-Hammer, a Bowling Green manufacturing plant for electrical components. The company was having labor issues at the time, and it was thought the blast was strike-related. Still, it showed dynamite was the choice of destruction.

Almost a year later, on September 26, 1969, a 600-foot television tower was destroyed by dynamite. WLTV had received several phone calls warning them to back off from their reporting of some of the crimes in the city. The tower was located thirteen miles northwest of Bowling Green. It knocked the station off the air for eleven days and caused an estimated damage of $250,000. Two cases of dynamite were used to bring the tower down.

In 1968–69 there had been a staggering thirty-two homicides in Warren County. Individuals had been shot, stabbed, died in burned-out cars and houses, and pulled from creeks and rivers. Compare that to the seven murders in the county in 2017. Was it any wonder the city's own residents referred to Bowling Green as "Little Chicago?"

It got so bad that one person who owned property along Barren River erected a sign that read "Positively No Dead Bodies Dumped in This Area."

In 1970, Sheriff Hubert Phelps told the local newspaper that police were getting calls at least once a month. "At first," he said, "when people find bodies lying beside the road, it was assumed it was a drunk."

The following summer, on June 15, 1970, dynamite blasted The Pub Tavern owned by Noah Cook on the 31-W ByPass. The bomb had been placed under one of the booths next to an exterior wall. Police found a clock-like mechanism and two dry cell batteries near the point of explosion.

The Pub's manager, Carlton Wiley, was injured in the blast. Later, Police Detective Sgt. Raymond Raymer told reporters he believed the blast contained from two to four sticks of dynamite.

Newspapers throughout Kentucky were reporting that more than a dozen dynamitings in Warren County had occurred over the past several years and that none had been solved. Only one man had been arrested, Billy Graham, and he was murdered before he went to trial.

CHAPTER NINE

A lull in the bombings gave Bowling Green a false sense of security. But, then on February 16, 1972, Det. Captain Darrell Moody's home was dynamited.

Moody had just walked out of his house on Henry Avenue where he lived with his wife and nine-year-old daughter. It was 8:24 a.m., and he had left earlier than usual to be a witness in a shoplifting case.

"I had been investigating a million dollar car theft ring for two years," Moody said at the time. "The people in it don't want to be put out of business, so they tried to kill me."

There had been some recent arrests in the case, and Moody said he thought the bombing was revenge, as well as intended to put a halt to the investigation.

Later the same day, Melvin Eugene Moore was killed ten miles north of London, Kentucky, in a gun battle with a state trooper that Moore wounded.

Bowling Green Police Chief Constant said evidence found on Moore's body and at his trailer home near Lexington linked him with a dynamite theft there and with the bombing of Moody's home. Chief Constant said more arrests would follow. Kenneth Wayne Taylor was that other person. Taylor died later that year in a gunfight with another man.

In December 1972, Detective Moody wasn't the only one targeted for getting too close to messing up somebody's criminal activities. Alabama had been a hotbed for stolen cars because of the state's haphazard rules that allowed easy registration.

In Scottsboro, Alabama, not far from Anniston, an attorney, Loy Campbell, was closing in. Dynamite blew both of his legs off, and because so little evidence remained, no one was arrested. Years later ATF Special Agent Bridgewater felt like some Bowling Green people had a hand in it.

A popular nightspot in Bowling Green, The Main Office Lounge, was the next victim of a dynamiting. On April 2,1973, explosives were tossed on the roof, causing $4,000 in damages. And then on June 22 of the same year, bartender David Devore had been tipped off that a bomb had been placed in a box behind the lounge. Immediately the lounge was evacuated, and city policeman Jim Rogers disarmed the live bomb. Rogers said the bomb consisted of a dynamite cap, black powder, flammable gas, a fuse, and an alarm clock.

Western Kentucky University was not immune to bomb scares either. In August 1973, a bomb was disarmed on the third floor of the seven-level parking structure. An anonymous phone call tipped the college off.

The rumors were rampant about midnight machine gunnings and hired gunmen from the North being sent to Bowling Green to kill the county's biggest alcohol wholesalers. Local citizens of influence formed a group and announced it was time for the violence to cease. More rewards were offered for pertinent information leading to arrest.

A multi-state car theft ring, headquartered in Bowling Green, had been operating at full throttle. It was the one Det. Darrell Moody was investigating when his house was blown up. The ring stretched into Tennessee, Alabama, and eight other states.

In the local Bowling Green news, however, much of the attention had been given to the success of the Western Kentucky Hilltopper basketball team that had reached a historic run to the Final Four in 1971.

The success of the car theft ring that began in 1968 depended on the ability to sell stolen cars that appeared, on all but the closest of examination, to have been legitimately acquired and registered. Papers of a wrecked automobile, as well as forged papers purportedly issued elsewhere, were presented to a county clerk to obtain new and seemingly valid papers matching the numbers and description of the stolen vehicle. This was made possible by the decentralized nature of the Kentucky registration system, whereby registrations were issued out of thirty-five different county clerk's offices. By constantly moving from county seat to county seat and appearing at rush hours, the possibility of detection was minimized.

Twenty-two individuals were indicted in August 1972. Among them was Billy D. Mayes, thirty-four, who according to court records was considered one of the masterminds.

William A. Hudson, known as Willie, was charged with offering $3,000 and later $5,000, to four men to kill an unidentified informant. A four-stick dynamite bomb was found in the informant's car on January 21, 1971, but did not explode.

Mayes and Larry Gann, twenty-five, of Bowling Green, were charged with discussing plans to kill Barry Lynn Clayton because he had helped the grand jury in the investigation.

Gann later died in a suspicious house fire in a burned-out trailer in September 2000.

To further show just how sophisticated and specialized the ring was, Claude Dillon Jr. testified that on Mayes' orders he stole cars of specific types and models, down to power steering, power brakes and air conditioning. Dillon said he got $250 for Volkswagens and $600 for Cadillacs. He went on to testify that he "could have anybody killed because I have some real wild hippie friends."

Forty-seven-year-old L. C. Cook was also indicted. He had not been one of the run-of-the-mill car thieves. He had a thirty-year career as a jockey, once winning the Kentucky Oaks in 1957. In the 1955 Kentucky Derby, he rode Trim Destiny to a tenth-place finish behind the winner, Swaps. In 1988, after threatening his ex-wife and shooting into her house in Louisville, she fired back and killed him. He was sixty-three.

On April 9, 1973, five witnesses for the U.S. government in U.S. district court testified they themselves stole some 1,800 cars over the last few years. They testified they were members of a "gang" based out of Bowling Green.

Claude Dillon Jr. testified he stole 500 cars; Barry Lynn Clayton, 500; C.W. Marcum, 300; James Cecil Wilson, 400; and Paul Bunton, 100.

Dillon also told the jury he had received a $60 weekly pension from the government for the past seven months for his cooperation and testimony.

During the trial all government witnesses admitted to being thieves. Barry Lynn Clayton said he had participated in car thefts with seventeen of the defendants. He told the court he had stolen lots of cars and even asked to join the ring.

"They knew I was worthy of their association," he said. "I contacted them, I broke the ice. I told them I wanted part of the action."

Clayton continued.

"I never stole a car from someone I didn't know. I stole only for insurance frauds. I would proposition a person and tell them I could get rid of their cars for the insurance money."

He said he would get $250-$300 from the owner of the car and then strip the vehicle or resell to members of the ring. He told the jury that Billy Mayes was head of the organization.

Marcum said he often stole cars from shopping centers in Louisville during daylight hours. "Nobody would suspect you of stealing cars in broad daylight."

He said he stole cars on the orders of Mayes, who paid him $400 for each car.

Witnesses came and went in the U.S. district court trial in Bowling Green. All eyes and ears were open among the jurors and the spectators who filled the court room. Anytime someone entered the courtroom, the heavy door squeaked, making a noise heard throughout the room. Every head would turn to see if it was a new witness or spectator entering.

The government introduced Fontis Emberton from Louisville, who said he found a four-stick dynamite bomb in his car on January 21, 1971. As a government witness, Emberton had a story to tell, but there were those who didn't want him to tell it.

It was later in the morning that Max J. Bayer took the witness stand to relate his knowledge of the bombing attempt on Emberton's life.

Bayer testified that he was hired by Shirley Basham and Willie Hudson, both from Bowling Green, to eliminate Emberton and keep him from testifying.

Bayer told everyone that the contract on Emberton carried a price of $3,000 but was later raised to $5,000. He further said he agreed to take the contract but did not fulfill the agreement.

According to a May 19, 1973, *Bowling Green Daily News* report, Melvin Eugene Moore placed the bomb in Emberton's car in 1971, and he was the same person alleged to have planted the bomb at Detective Darrell Moody's house in February 1972.

By accounts from newspapers ranging from Indianapolis, to Cincinnati, to Birmingham, to Knoxville, to Nashville, to Louisville, and, of course to Bowling Green, Billy Mayes, Shirley Basham, and Willie Hudson were the masterminds of the car theft ring. And on May 24,

1973, U.S. District Judge Mac Swinford sentenced the alleged ringleader Mayes to five years in prison and a $10,000 fine.

The jury had deliberated nine hours over two days after listening to eight weeks of testimony.

At the conclusion, twenty-two of those indicted had gone to trial, with nineteen found guilty and three acquitted.

In his closing comments, Judge Swinford referred to the car theft operation as a "very significant and big enterprise. It's amazing to me that some of these people have done nothing in their lives but violate the law."

One person who did not want to be identified said one of the car theft ring members told him, "I can make three or four hundred thousand dollars, hide it in my backyard, and do eight or nine months (in prison). I can't make that kind of money doing it the other way. I'm willing to serve time for that kind of money."

By all outward appearances, Police Chief Wayne Constant was doing everything he could to curb the violence. His cadre of policemen were unable to keep up with the growing violence and homicides in the city and county. Policemen in Bowling Green numbered just below thirty throughout the '50s; in the '60s, they increased to forty-five; and by the '70s, their numbers were close to sixty.

Chief Constant had a history of law enforcement, at one time serving as a Warren County deputy sheriff. It was then that in 1954, Constant was arrested and charged with two others for dynamiting fish in the Barren River. The two others were Deputy Constable Emory Gaines and friend Walter "June Bug" Simpson, a known gambler who had a history of liquor violations. Constant was suspended by Warren County Sheriff Carl Jordon.

How ironic it was with all the dynamite issues in Bowling Green, a story in the *Louisville Courier Journal* on July 23, 1967, Sunday edition featured Police Chief Constant looking over a dog's "paw-print signature" on a bank check.

According to the story, the nine-year-old dog's paw print was legal. The check was drawn on from a bank in Scottsville, Kentucky, for the purpose of paying for a Bowling Green parking ticket. Oh yes, the name of the dog ... "Miss Dynamite."

On May 23, 1974, a mobile home sales office was bombed for no apparent reason on the northside of the 31-W ByPass between Ray's Drive Inn Restaurant and the Sunset Inn, a bar in Bowling Green.

At 11:30 p.m. someone had placed a Pringles potato chip can stuffed with dynamite inside of a milk carton and blew up the Park City Mobile Home sales office.

It just so happened that several times in the days before the bombing, Billy Mayes, who was back on the streets of Bowling Green again, dropped by the sales office to have some papers notarized by an employee. Owner Oscar "Buckshot" Belcher wasn't really happy that Mayes was there.

Belcher said he came into his office one day, and Mayes was there. "I came in about half mad or something, and I said, 'looks like all the car thieves hang out at my business,' and that was the extent of it. Really, I didn't think much about it at the time. He left."

Little did Belcher realize he had said the wrong thing to Mayes.

Mayes contacted Steve Leo Monroe, a twenty-three-year-old who was already on a fast track to prison. In 1970, Monroe had a brief stint in the Marine Corps but got in trouble for stealing a car while stationed at San Diego Marine Recruit Depot in California and taking it across the state line into Arizona. He was assigned to a Correctional Custody Unit, where it would be decided if his service to his country could be salvaged. He was soon discharged. The son of a well-known Bowling Green businessman, Beryl Monroe, Steve had married at nineteen, had a son, divorced, and remarried. But already he had begun to build a criminal résumé. It went from petty stuff to stealing cars with his friend, Carlos Lloyd.

"Our specialty was pickup trucks," said Lloyd. "But we stole Cadillacs and Corvettes, too. We'd work on altering the numbers and then sell them to Billy Mayes and Larry Gann."

The relationship between Billy Mayes and Steve Monroe went beyond stealing cars. Mayes also knew that Monroe knew how to blow things up. After all, Steve's dad's A-Monroe Rent-All business dealt in construction work that would sometime involve dynamite, and Monroe had been a part of it.

Mayes struck a deal with Monroe to get revenge on Buckshot Belcher for the offensive comment Belcher had made to him several days earlier.

Bowling Green policeman Gary Raymer, an eight-year veteran at the time, who would later become the city's police chief, was the first law enforcement officer on the scene that night. He knew almost immediately that it was dynamite.

"There was a distinct odor about the whole trailer that exploded," he said. "And I'd smelled this odor before."

Four previous times he had arrived at the scene of dynamite explosions in Bowling Green, Raymer said, and immediately he put in a call to local ATF Special Agent Bob Bridgewater.

Bridgewater was a physical presence, tall, with dark skin that left little doubt he came from Native American heritage. Within ten minutes he arrived at the explosion site, ready to do what he was supposed to do.

With twelve-and-a-half years as a Special Agent, Bridgewater smelled the same odor—dynamite. He took pictures while trying to determine at what point the explosive was placed. After a while it was determined that the bomb had been placed above the trailer's rear axle. Small parts of an alarm clock that had been used as the timing element were found. Bridgewater estimated six to seven sticks of dynamite had been used. An extensive search of the bomb scene continued into the next day.

"There was a pretty sizable crowd watching us working the crime scene," Raymer said. "Some of them started throwing rocks at us while we were sifting through all of the stuff."

The crime scene, however, was about to reveal even more.

CHAPTER TEN

E nough evidence was finally put together to arrest Steve Monroe for the bombing in Bowling Green. ATF Special Agent Bob Bridgewater made the arrest on June 25, 1974. He knew who Monroe was. He had seen him walking around the Park City Mobile Home parking lot after the blast. Police officer Gary Raymer had seen him, too, and told Bridgewater who Monroe was.

"When I arrested him, he wanted to be a little confrontational," remembered Bridgewater. "I said, look, we can do it your way or do it my way, how do you want it? He said, 'Your way.'"

Agent Bridgewater was a big man no one in their right mind would want to tangle with.

Monroe was booked, fingerprinted, and locked up. But only for a brief period. His dad, Beryl Monroe, leveraged his rental business and posted bail for his son.

Jimmy Brown had been a friend of Monroe's since the two were teenagers. Both had been in and out of petty trouble, but Brown had recently worked with Monroe at Atlas Transmission Shop, a business owned by Monroe's dad.

It was here that Steve Monroe was managing the shop, and Brown was one of the mechanics. On May 22, Brown was informed by Monroe that he had a job for him to do and needed him to return to the transmission shop around 7 or 7:30 that night. Monroe, without hesitating, told him a trailer on 31-W ByPass needed to be dynamited. Brown agreed to do the job, and the two proceeded to build the bomb with unwrapped dynamite that Brown provided.

It was not the first time Brown had worked with Monroe in constructing destructive devices, as both knew how it was done. This time nine sticks of dynamite were tamped into a Pringles potato chip canister, and a Westclox Baby Ben clock mechanism was added to make the cap explode at a predetermined time. Dynamite caps, two size C batteries to detonate the bomb were used, and then to test it, they wired a flashlight bulb to the circuit that led to the dynamite's cap. It was ready.

All the while the two had painted the windows black in the shop to make sure no one could see them making the bomb.

Monroe and Brown headed out to Park City Mobile Home office from the Russellville Road transmission shop to place the bomb. With the lights still on in the office, they decided to go have a drink at the Little Brown Jug, a nearby bar. A little later Monroe asked Brown to drive him home and then for him to go back and set the bomb.

Giving Monroe several excuses, Brown did not place the bomb and, the next morning, carried it back into the transmission shop, where Monroe hid it in the dirty uniform clothes hamper.

Ronnie Klokoc was another employee at Atlas, and he saw the bomb. The next day on May 23, Billy Mayes came by and Monroe showed him the bomb, telling him, "This should do the job."

Mayes had paid Monroe $500 and wanted results. At first Klokoc thought the bomb might be for him, but Brown assured him it was not, only adding to the distrust of bad guys who do bad things.

Monroe once again told Brown to place the bomb that night, but once again, Brown found a way to get out of it. Since Brown did not meet Monroe at the designated time at the transmission shop, Monroe took it on himself to retrieve the bomb from his shop.

Monroe was friends with Ronald "Stormy" Stronk.. Stronk was a session player in Nashville but played music all over Bowling Green, including at the Main Office Lounge, College Street Inn, the Spot, and the Sunset Inn next door to the Park City Mobile Homes. Over the years Stronk had off and on rented a trailer at Beryl Monroe's trailer park.

Stronk's reputation was not the best. By Stronk's own account, Bowling Green Police Detective Fred Lancaster "wanted my butt so bad he could taste it. I was into some drugs back then. I sold it for $80 a kilo … dirt cheap. I've lost several years of my memory."

In December 2018, an answering recorder at Stronk's residence in South Carolina advised callers, "Never retreat … always reload … and remember, incoming fire has the right of way … God bless you … bye."

The Sunset Inn was a frequent hangout of Monroe's, a *Cheers*-type place where everybody knew his name and he knew theirs. He was so comfortable there that he could walk in drinking a beer that he brought with him.

The nightspot was a blend of college students and locals there for the entertainment. The lounge had a bit of Wild West atmosphere in that it was loud and customers would go in and out with their drinks and even go behind the bar. And when he wasn't drinking beer, Monroe's choice of drinks was an Old Fashioned.

The owner of the Sunset Inn, Bob Hereford, had his own run-in with the law later in 1978. Hereford and seven others were arrested in connection with fourteen burglaries in four counties over several months.

That night, on May 23, Stronk was driving his new 1974 Pontiac Grand Prix and picked up Monroe at his house, unaware that he was driving him by the shop to get a bomb. From there they headed to the Sunset Inn, where eventually Monroe was able to slip over to the mobile home sales lot next door and place the explosive.

The explosion was so loud and forceful that it emptied the two local bars next door as customers spilled out into the parking lots to see what had happened. Soon cop cars and fire trucks were everywhere.

Monroe knew the bomb would be loud. In fact, he told Klokoc, who lived in the same neck of the woods as Park City Mobile Homes, "That if he heard an explosion about 11:30 p.m. and sees Buckshot's (Belcher) head rolling down the road, don't think anything about it."

Klokoc, like Brown, knew all about the sideline business Steve Monroe was in. They, too, had been right there with him.

Klokoc's story included knowingly receiving stolen property, grand larceny, and construction jobs where he worked with dynamite.

He had known Monroe since his family moved to Bowling Green when Steve was fifteen. The two had joined the Marine Corps in the same year.

"I was sixteen and Steve was seventeen, I think," Klokoc said in later years. "I went to Vietnam, and he didn't. He told everybody he was wounded in Vietnam and would show an appendectomy scar."

Jimmy Brown seemed to stay in trouble with the law, no matter what state he lived in. After moving to Michigan, he literally set up his own cottage industry by burglarizing vacation homes, hunting lodges, and anything else he could get into. And then he got involved with several others, which led to his connection to three murders in Michigan, one that included a police officer.

Monroe and his associates seemed to have lots of experience with dynamite. The front to it was blasting rock in legitimate construction , but beneath the surface they used that experience and turned it into terrorism. That's what bombs were in Bowling Green—terroristic threats. Many times the bombs become more than threats.

For Steve Monroe, dynamite was readily available to him, not through Atlas Transmission's but A-Monroe Rent-All. Steve's father, Beryl, rented lots of construction equipment that would sometimes require dynamite, so these explosives became part of his inventory.

The one place in Bowling Green that was a federally licensed dealer of dynamite was Gale's Distributors. And owner Gale Stiles did quite a bit of business with A-Monroe Rent-All.

Anyone who purchased explosives from Stiles was required by law to fill out Form 4710 and sign it. On January 19, 1973, Steve L. Monroe purchased fifty-pounds of Hercules gelatin-based explosives and signed the form, listing himself as part-owner of his dad's business.

Monroe had access to all the dynamite he needed. Some, of course, was used legitimately to blast rock for a water line or for blowing up tree stumps to install a septic tank. But some was also used for Monroe's other jobs.

Steve Leo Monroe didn't just decide to steal cars and blow up things over night. Bowling Green lawmen felt like he was involved in a lot more than just blowing up a trailer sales office, but, keep in mind, explosions don't leave much evidence.

CHAPTER ELEVEN

Sometime in 1973, Steve Monroe met Carlos Lloyd through an introduction by Lloyd's younger brother. Lloyd was twenty-seven and looking for a job.

Even though Monroe was three years younger than Lloyd, his reputation that he was into stealing cars and selling them to Billy Mayes and Larry Gann had spread among the Bowling Green underworld.

"I needed a job and some fast money," Lloyd said. "And to me stealing a car was nothing more than a job. I needed the money. I wanted to buy a house. My wife and I were separated, and she said if we could buy a house, we could get back together. We had two girls and a boy."

Lloyd's specialty was stealing pickup trucks, but he was open to any and all, if the opportunity presented itself. Since he was always ready, his friends knew he kept a key-making machine in the trunk of his car. All he needed was a serial or VIN number.

"My first car was a 1972 Cadillac I stole in Nashville," he said. "I drove it a little crazy, and Larry Gann wasn't real happy with me. He was probably concerned I'd be stopped by the police. Steve and I stole two Corvettes and drove them to Clearwater, Florida, and sold them to a guy who use to live in Bowling Green but had moved there to open a used car business."

Lloyd didn't have the best of a home life growing up, being the middle child of four brothers and two sisters. His dad's schooling went to the second grade and his mother's to the eighth. She worked at Union Underwear, and his father was a house painter.

"I had no direction at home," he said. "The only thing my dad ever said was 'never cuss in front of me.' We were hunting and I said, 'Look, there's a damn squirrel in that tree.' He hit me so hard it knocked me out."

School was just a place to spend time as far as Lloyd was concerned.

"I hated school," he said. "I spent two years in the sixth grade and three in the seventh. I quit school when I was fourteen."

Lloyd's first real trouble came at sixteen. He was at a time in his life that it was up to him to make good or bad decisions. No longer in school, so whatever influence a teacher might have had on him was now out of the picture. Most of his decisions would be influenced by the friends he kept, one of which was Howard D. Causey.

"H. D. and I broke into a house in Bowling Green and stole a bunch of coins," said Lloyd. "We got caught because they (police) were able to track the coins when I tried to spend some of the silver dollars we stole. Got a year probation on that one."

For many, a brush with breaking and entering and a light slap on the wrist might have been enough to turn a life in another direction. But for Carlos Lloyd, it had little effect.

"We tried to break into a service station one night," he said. "We were crawling through a window when the police came. We ran and never got caught. It showed us we could get away."

Ultimately things didn't work out well for his friend, Causey. Causey's crime-filled youth eventually landed him in jail and then on to Indiana State Prison, where he died of stab wounds in a prison disturbance in 1972. He was twenty-five.

The relationship between Lloyd and Monroe, in their world, seemed like a match made in heaven. They had begun to live by their own rules early in life. By all appearances Monroe's family seemed more grounded, in that Beryl Monroe, Steve's father, had a successful business and, by all accounts, was a hard-working man. He wanted the best for his son, and when Beryl invested in a transmission shop and gave Steve the management responsibility, it seemed Steve Monroe had a bright future.

Monroe and Lloyd soon formed an unwritten partnership. Monroe needed more than a transmission shop, and Lloyd needed money in order to put his family back together financially. To them, stealing cars and trucks was a means to an end.

"We were tough badasses, at least we thought we were," Lloyd offered. "We partied, stayed drunk, and stole cars."

There were times Monroe would be gone for a week or two from his transmission shop, working his second job.

"It didn't take long for several cars and trucks to be setting outside of our building with Alabama license plates," recalled employee, Ronnie Klokoc. "I never knew for sure if they were stolen or not. I do know we had a backhoe on our lot that Steve had stolen."

In 1974, Atlas Transmission went out of business, and this left Monroe without a place to work on their cars and build their bombs.

Lloyd and Monroe found some property on 31-W south, just at the edge of Bowling Green to rent. It was 126 acres, consisting of a house, garage, shed, and two large barns. It wasn't the land they were interested in, just the buildings.

Lloyd signed the rental agreement with the property's owner, Neal Turner, who was president of Western Realty, one of Bowling Green's largest real estate firms. The $200 monthly rental was for the house and garage, and Lloyd and Monroe moved in on December 16, 1974.

"This is where we worked on the cars we were stealing, where we'd weld over the old frames and change all of the numbers," Lloyd said. "Then we'd sell them to Gann and Mayes."

Since Lloyd was keeping up with his rent, Turner (nor anyone else) paid attention to what buildings were being used. All Turner knew was that he was paid again on January 16, 1975, which secured the property for Lloyd and Monroe to February 16.

Turner wasn't sure what buildings on his property the two car thieves were using, but by Lloyd's account they used more than just the house and garage.

Lloyd's "front" job had been working construction in Bowling Green. Even though he hated school, he was talented in things other than stealing cars. He had become proficient in building houses.

"I could do plumbing, electrical, anything that involved construction," he said. "It was hard work, but I needed more money, and the cars were easy."

For Steve Leo Monroe and Carlos Calvin Lloyd, their lives were about to reach another level.

Enter David Cooper Walker.

CHAPTER TWELVE

D avid Cooper Walker was well known in Bowling Green circles. With highly respected parents, Edgar and Irene, doors opened easily for him.

The Walkers were one of the wealthiest families in Warren County, and their real estate holdings were among the largest. It hadn't always been that way, however.

Edgar had been an auctioneer for twenty years in Macon, Missouri, a small town a couple of hours north of St. Louis, before he decided to move his family, along with their pony, to Bowling Green, Kentucky, in 1935. He sold his cattle, loaded his furniture in a cattle truck, and headed to Kentucky.

Col. Walker, as he was called, had owned the Macon Auction Company. However, a by-chance visit to Bowling Green on some cattle business opened his eyes to some business opportunities he didn't have back in Missouri. But a few years before that move, Edgar and wife Irene began to build their family.

In February 1930, Edgar and Irene Walker went to an orphanage in St. Charles, Missouri, with hopes of adopting a little redheaded girl. But when a small nine-month-old little boy pulled himself up to the side of his crib, he caught Irene's eye. "This is the one that needs me," she said, quickly pausing at the crib.

It was then that the young boy became David Cooper Walker. Always called David Cooper by family members because of Irene's maiden name, while he may not have been born with the proverbial silver spoon in his mouth, he had one now.

Even at an early age David Walker had developed a knack for finding trouble. While visiting his grandmother in Macon, Missouri, in 1943, he was arrested driving a 1935 Plymouth he had stolen in a nearby town.

That same year, the local *Macon Missouri Chronicle* reported that David C. Walker was involved in a car theft in which he stole his grandmother's car and took it on a "two day pleasure spree" to several nearby communities. He was fourteen.

Walker attended Columbia Military Academy in Tennessee in the early 40s before running away and enlisting in the Navy. Only fifteen, he forged his parents' signature, claiming he was seventeen. He had retrieved enough history out of the family Bible to give credibility to his age. He had told his friends he was mad at the Japanese for bombing Pearl Harbor.

Even though he was assigned to the USS *Nevada*, his military career didn't last long. A dishonorable discharge sent him back to Bowling Green.

He had been in the Navy long enough, however, to befriend a fellow seaman on the USS *Nevada* named Norman Hudson. Hudson had become disengaged from his own family and would write to and receive letters from David's mother, Irene. After the Navy, Hudson moved to Bowling Green, went to work for Edgar Walker in the real estate business, and eventually became successful in his own right.

By now the Walker family had purchased sixty-some acres of land at the edge of Bowling Green in 1948, with plans to build a home and move from their Sumpter Avenue residence.

Known as Cemetery Pike, Edgar and Irene built a stately home that became known as Walkerhurst. With its long driveway and large columns, the house could easily be seen from the main road and was a topic of conversation around not just Bowling Green but Warren County as well.

Edgar Walker had become the owner of the Bowling Green Stockyards, purchased the old fairgrounds at the corner of the ByPass and Cemetery Road, and later helped develop what became known as Fairview Plaza Shopping Center on the property. When Edgar and Irene later sold off the property, they carved out a parcel of the shopping center for son David, so that he would always have income from it. They also owned hundreds of acres elsewhere in the city and county.

David Walker shuffled in and out of trouble, of which some of it was blamed on the fact that he found out from a friend, while visiting his grandmother in Missouri, that he was adopted. He resented that he had not been told by his parents.

It seemed there was always someone making excuses for his behavior. His mother, Irene, was described as a stern taskmaster, not a warm, loving person when it came to family. At times she would try to reel her son in when he got into trouble. Her husband, Edgar, on the other hand, was quick to use his money and social status in Bowling Green to get David out of trouble. It was Irene's opinion that her husband only added to David's problems by making it easier for him. Wealth did not, however, keep Irene Walker from stopping her car and picking up Coke bottles tossed on the side of the road from time to time.

A *Louisville Courier-Journal* article in September 1955 printed that twenty-six-year-old David C. Walker had been indicted along with two others for dwelling house breaking and attempted safe breaking. Once again his parents and their high-priced Bowling Green lawyers got him off.

It was a consensus among law enforcement in Bowling Green that if David Walker was involved in anything, it was probably bad. One former police officer said David opened a photography studio to take pictures of beautiful young girls; another said he rented space on the second floor of an office building directly across from the courthouse in downtown Bowling Green, where he ran illegal high-stakes card games. His reputation was such that he would randomly be searched for a concealed weapon.

Walker's name again appeared in the *Courier-Journal* in the September 2, 1963, edition when the state of Kentucky published a monthly list of drivers who had lost their driver's license while driving intoxicated.

It didn't have to be that way, as his parents tried to steer him in the right direction, but with zero results. They thought he might be getting his life together when on June 25, 1966, he married an attractive young girl on one of his visits to Alabama for who knows what. She was eighteen and he was thirty-seven.

He brought his wife back to Bowling Green, where they lived in a small apartment in the rear of Walkerhurst on Cemetery Road.

Although Walker's education had been spotty, he was able to enroll in 1966 at Western Kentucky University. He decided he wanted to major in business, and finally take over the management of his mother and father's vast real estate holdings. But all of that was short-lived.

"He lost interest in things quickly," his wife said. "He had multiple personalities, and I never knew which one I was going to get. The good

David was consumed by the bad David. I was so vulnerable to his actions, and I'm ashamed to say it, but I loved him and feared him at the same time."

The drug culture was just beginning to take hold on college campuses across America, and Western Kentucky University in Bowling Green was no different. There were those who recalled that Walker, who enrolled as a student in 1966, was involved in that, too.

Norman Hudson, who the Walker family had befriended, knew what David Walker was up to.

"My dad told Walker he'd better stay away from me," Hudson's son Alan said. "David would show up at music events on campus dressed sort of like a hippie and make his contacts in the parking lot at the dorms."

ATF Agent Bob Bridgewater also said Walker was involved in the early drug days around Bowling Green.

"Law enforcement kept an eye on him if anything out of the ordinary was going on," Bridgewater added.

Former Warren County Sheriff Jerry "Peanut" Gaines knew the Walker family well. It was his father who had helped move the Walkers in a big cattle truck from Missouri to Bowling Green years before.

"David had a smart criminal mind," Gaines said. "He had lots of personality, that coal black hair, and always wanted to be a gangster."

Walker developed a friendship and partnership with David Dennison, who, like Walker, ran afoul of the law periodically. The two were always in search of something "to get into."

One of those searches involved a trip to St. Louis on August 15, 1968, to look at a horse track. With all the real estate holdings the Walkers had, finding suitable land for a horse track around Bowling Green would be no problem.

Walker and Dennison hired Horace Brown, a building contractor who owned his own plane, to fly them over to look around. On approach to East Side Airport, Brown's aircraft quickly lost altitude, crash landed, and flipped over in a muddy field, causing extensive damage to the plane. All three were taken to St. Mary's Hospital in East St. Louis.

It was Brown, according to his son, who saw his dad show Walker how to take a pencil and poke a hole in the end of a dynamite stick and put a blasting cap in it and tape it together.

"My dad had me to run out to his truck and get a couple of sticks, so he could show David," said his son, who was a young boy at the time.

David Walker's engaging personality was such that he was able to meander his way into a multitude of acquaintanceships, if not friendships. Always operating on the fringes of breaking the law, he took comfort that his mother and father would cover for him. His father, Edgar, died in 1967, and now his mother, Irene, was going to make sure that David was financially taken care of, along with his adopted sister, Polly, who lived in California.

Before Edgar Walker died, he donated an organ to the First Christian Church in Bowling Green. He also gave the church some property behind Fairview Plaza Shopping Center, but shortly after his death, Irene sued the church to get the property back. She won the suit.

By now, David and his wife had three children.

"David lived in another world," she said. "He never confided with us on anything. He was a control freak when it came to our family."

According to her there were times men would come to their house looking for David. "I had no idea who they were or what they wanted. It was scary."

Walker's notoriety was not just in Bowling Green. Surrounding counties were aware of who he was, and some of the things he could get done for a price.

David Cooper Walker might be able to escape the law, but he couldn't escape himself.

CHAPTER THIRTEEN

Russellville, in Logan County, might have more beautiful, charming historic homes for its size than any town in Kentucky. With a population of 7,000, the residential district has some 200 homes that date back to 1815 to 1940, and the town has produced four Kentucky governors; a governor each in Illinois, Texas and Florida; five U.S. Senators; six congressmen; three Kentucky Chief Justices; three U.S. Ambassadors; three federal Cabinet officers; and four men who died at the Alamo, among them the legendary Jim Bowie.

As illustrious as history is to Logan County, the same can also be said for its politics. A hard-charging county that leaned heavily Democratic, few would challenge the "machine" led by Emerson "Doc" Beauchamp. An endorsement by Doc most often meant victory.

There was, however, a man raised in the Logan County community of Auburn who had the ambition to someday be the county's sheriff. Jim Johnson publicly said he always wanted to "come back home" and be the sheriff. But for sure he took a roundabout way of going for it.

Johnson, raised mostly by his grandparents, had left high school early to join the Navy, where he earned his high school diploma. After three years in the Navy, he applied for and was accepted into the Kentucky State Police.

Assigned to Post 4 in Elizabethtown, he rose to the rank of sergeant, and not content to just put in his hours, Johnson became active in the creation of Trooper Island, a Kentucky State Police-sponsored retreat at Lake Cumberland for kids across Kentucky.

Jim Johnson had a drive to him, a gift for gab and met people easily, and as he neared retirement after sixteen-and-a-half years, he went to Dusty Rhodes, the Ford dealer in Elizabethtown, and asked if he could sell cars part-time for him.

He knew Dusty because all the state troopers drove Fords, and the dealership did all of their service work. The two had become friends, and Dusty thought it would be a good fit. Dusty's way of thinking was, if it worked out, Johnson might want to come on full-time after he retired.

But for Jim Johnson's way of thinking, it was a way to make some extra money while also learning about the automobile business. He was no different from a lot of people—he wanted to make money and be successful.

By 1966, Harold Kitchens had purchased the Ford dealership in Russellville, and was looking for someone to come aboard as a partner and to run the business. Kitchens was known as a good businessman. A lot of his business was accomplished with partnerships, one of which was done several years earlier with Edgar Walker in owning the Bowling Green Stockyards.

With Johnson in the process of leaving the state police, what better way for him to return home? A deal was worked out, and soon a sign went up in the Bethel Shopping Center: "Johnson-Kitchens Ford." Johnson's ambition and foresight in hooking up with Dusty Rhodes paid off.

Ken Gilliam was thirty-one years old when he joined them as the dealership's service manager, so he got to know Johnson well. He saw his ambition of wanting to put a Ford in every Logan County driveway.

Over the next couple of years, Gilliam and Johnson made several trips together, conducting business and staying in contact with old friends whom Johnson had made in Elizabethtown and Frankfort within the hierarchy of the Kentucky State Police.

A stop at Johnson's old workplace, Post 4 in Elizabethtown, to say hello and shake a few hands is something he did on a regular basis. It was here that Gilliam met Sgt. Eugene Coffey, who ten years later became semi-famous for killing Clyde Graham in a motel room in Effingham, Illinois. Graham was believed to have shot and killed Trooper Eddie Harris in 1979. Sgt. Coffey tracked Graham for over a month before shooting him. Coffey always maintained Graham was reaching for a weapon when he fired on him in what turned out to be a controversial investigation of the shooting.

Gilliam said even then, in the late '60s, Coffey's reputation was that he could take people out.

This sign near Old Richardsville Road northwest of Bowling Green was found after a gambler was murdered dumped there in 1970, the third body found there in as many months.

Alcohol raid in Logan County.

John "Buster" Johnson, 1950s.

Marshal Ray Shaw examines beer that was seized in Russellville.

Raided alcohol in Logan County.

Legion Post Raided By State, Sheriff; Slots, Beer Seized

Legion Post Raided headline.

Jim Johnson (left) and fellow lawman toss raided beer.

Sheriff In Liquor Raid At Olmstead

Sheriff in Liquor Raid headline.

Jim Johnson with the Kentucky State Police

Candidates for Office

The News-Democrat and the Logan Leader are authorized to announce the following persons as candidates for the various offices of Logan County and the Commonwealth of Kentucky, subject to the Primary Election May 27, 1969.

City Judge
Les Newberry
Michael Stratton

Sheriff
L. C. Kees
Raymond L. Hollingsworth
William E. Gorrell
Jimmy Johnson

County Surveyor
William A. Norris

Tax Commissioner
(Property Valuation Administrator)
Karl M. Dawson

County Judge
Bob Brown

City of Russellville

Mayor
Wallace Herndon

Council
Johnny Edwards
O. C. Gorham
John H. Guion, III
Thomas (Tom) Rhea, Jr
Eugene C. Riley
Harvey Smith

Jailer
Fount B. Shifflett
Joe Gunn Gregory
Bill Ed Soyars

House of

List of candidates for the Logan County offices in the election of May 1969, with four men running for sheriff.

VOTE FOR

JIM JOHNSON FOR SHERIFF

A

NEW

BROOM

SWEEPS

CLEAN

Vote For Experience — Vote For Qualifications!

JIM JOHNSON . . .

* Is a member of the Masonic Lodge #212.
* Is a member of the First Baptist Church.
* Is a Navy Veteran of World War II.
* Has never obligated himself to any political faction.

Newspaper advertisement for Jim Johnson, candidate for Sheriff, 1969.

Jim Johnson celebrates his win in the Sheriff's race.

Edgar and Irene Walker and son David Cooper Walker.

Irene Walker

Carlos Lloyd

David Cooper Walker, Western Kentucky University Yearbook, 1966.

Steve Monroe, high school sophomore year, 1968.

Steve L. Monroe

Bob and Thelma Bridge-water on their wedding day.

Bob Bridgewater

Blast Shatters Residence
Of City Police Detective

By TOM PATTERSON
Daily News Staff Writer

An early morning explosion heavily damaged a residence at 1310 Henry Ave. owned by Bowling Green Detective Capt. Darrell Moody.

No one was injured in the 8:24 apparent dynamite explosion which appeared to come from under the living room of the brick house.

Moody had left the house seconds before and had just entered his car when the explosion rocked the area. His wife, a waitress at Ray's Drive-In was at work and Moody's 9-year-old step-daughter was on her way to school, about a block from the house.

Moody, who stood shaking in front of the house shortly after the explosion, said he hadn't even started his car when the explosion occurred. "I called the police station on my car phone," he said. Moody's blue Oldsmobile was still parked about 50 feet in front of the house with debris scattered around it. Moody said he had no idea who might have blown up the house.

Bowling Green firemen were at the scene four minutes after the explosion was reported and immediately turned off gas and water lines to the house, then called the Electric Plant Board and had the power turned off leading into the house, according to city fire Maj. Harold Hazelip. No fire resulted from the explosion.

Hazelip said the main thrust of the explosion came directly under the living room and "there was a strong possibility it was a dynamite explosion. When we got here there was a strong dynamite smell all around the house," Hazelip said.

Federal officers were at the scene and Hazelip said the investigation had been turned over to them. Bob Bridgewater, an investigator with the treasury department, was taking pictures of the house and confirmed that a federal crew will be taking over the investigation. "It's a federal offense and they will be going

Continued on Back Page, Column 3, This Section

(Staff Photo by Paul Hightower)
LIVING ROOM DEMOLISHED — What was once the living room in the home of Bowling Green Detective Capt. Darrell Moody is almost unidentifiable after an apparent dynamite explosion went off under the house shortly after 8 a.m. today. No one was injured in the blast, which rocketed a portion of a living room couch into the attic.

House Is Blasted

Continued from page 1

over the house with a tooth and comb for any clues," he said.

Moody, a veteran of the Bowling Green Police Department was on his way to work at the time of the explosion, which rocked houses several blocks away. The inside of the house was hit worse by the explosion. Portions of a living room sofa were pushed into the attic from the blast, and many of the walls were shattered. Nearly all of the wooden living room floor had been shredded like toothpicks. Nearly all the bricks were blown off the house by the blast.

Most of the houses in the neighborhood of Moody's home have open access to the basements. A small cement leeway centered directly in the back of Moody's house would have given anyone access to the four-foot high basement, simply by opening a wooden door.

Most of Moody's neighbors were not home at the time of the explosion. However, Mrs. Robert Thomason, who lives next door to the Moody home said her husband was home in bed when the explosion occurred and he said their house shook and felt like it was coming down.

James Ray Bunch, who rents a house to Terry Thomas across the street from the Moody home said there was some damage done to the house. "There are several cracks in the ceiling and some cracks in the walls," he said.

Within an hour after the explosion City police had roped off the entire area around Moody's house and workman from Western Kentucky Gas Co. were checking the area for any broken lines which may have resulted from the explosion.

Home Destroyed

(Staff Photo by Paul Hightower)
SURVEY DAMAGE — Bowling Green Detective Capt. Darrell Moody and his wife Betty grimly survey the aftermath of a morning explosion, which destroyed their home located at 1310 Henry Ave. No one was injured in the 8:24 explosion.

(Staff Photo by Paul Hightower)
INVESTIGATION UNDERWAY — Treasury Investigator Bob Bridgewater, left, and City Detective Maj. Harry Ashby look over some of the damage caused by an explosion this morning at the home of Bowling Green Detective Capt. Darrell Moody. The investigation has been turned over to federal officials.

Dynamite Suspected

(Staff Photo by Paul Hightower)
HEAVILY DAMAGED — Scattered bricks and curtains which were blown out of the windows are evidence of an explosion in the home of Bowling Green Detective Capt. Darrell Moody shortly after 8 a.m. today. Moody had left the house seconds before the apparent dynamite explosion went off. His nine-year-old step-daughter had left the house a few minutes earlier. The explosion rocked houses within several blocks of the Moody home located at 1310 Henry Ave. No one was injured.

Newspaper stories covering the blast at Detective Darrell Moody's house

Hazy weekend

SOUTHCENTRAL KENTUCKY — Fair and warm tonight, low in the low 70s. Saturday partly cloudy and hazy, continued very warm and humid, high in mid 90s. Sunday continued hazy, warm and humid.

118 YEAR—NO. 195

PARK CITY

Daily News

BOWLING GREEN, KENTUCKY   FRIDAY, AUGUST 18, 1972

Auto theft investigation

Eight more arrested

By ROGER MILLER
Daily News Staff Writer

Eight more persons were arrested Thursday afternoon in connection with a 10-state car theft ring, bringing the number of arrests to 23 Thursday.

FBI agents said they believe the ring, based in Bowling Green, may be smashed, but local agent Marvin Baker said today, "This could be just the start of something bigger."

A sealed indictment returned Tuesday by the U.S. District Court grand jury named 28 persons in connection with auto thefts which have occurred in the last three years.

Only one person is being actively sought by the FBI. He is William Henry Wilson, 19, of Louisville.

He was believed by officers to be in Louisville Thursday night.

Three others named in indictments have been listed as fugitives since the grand jury began its lengthy investigation three months ago.

The three are Robert Wayne Murray, also known as Robert Parker and Kenneth H. Singletary, and Donald Ray Ellis and Kenneth Wayne Taylor. Their whereabouts are unknown.

The remaining person indicted, William Belvy Barbee, of Park City, was not sought by a federal warrant. A criminal summons was issued, and Barbee was recognized on his own bond of $2,000.

The 28 were charged with conspiracy to steal and transport in interstate commerce based on forged or stolen car registrations, and the interstate transportation of stolen vehicles and the concealment of stolen vehicles.

The 48-page indictment, opened Thursday, named an additional 13 persons as conspirators.

Several of the defendants and conspirators are charged with conspiring to murder possible witnesses and insurance fraud.

Fifteen of those arrested are from Warren County.

Those indicted are charged with the theft of more than 80 cars in the past three years.

Bond hearings were scheduled to be conducted at 2 p.m. today for those arrested.

Those arrested Thursday afternoon and their bonds before the 2 p.m. hearing were:

—Shirley Basham, 39, Bowling Green, cattleman and bondsman,

—Chester Crawley Scottsville, 48, arrested in Somerset, a farmer, $50,000.

—Larry Dale Gann, 25, Bowling Green, a refrigeration employe, $20,000.

—James Hendricks, 29, of Bowling Green, arrested in Indianapolis, truck driver, $100,000.

—Lewis Bewley, 30, Temple Hill, truck driver, $10,000.

—Ernest Frank Fowler, 38, formerly of Scottsville, arrested in Little Rock, Ark., formerly a manufacturing plant worker.

—Larry Osborn, no age listed, Chandler, Ariz., formerly with the U.S. Air Force, $10,000.

—Charles Adams, 47, Bowling Green, state supervisor of Gate Oil Co., $10,000.

One of the fugitives, Kenneth Wayne Taylor, earlier was indicted on charges of conspiring to dynamite a dwelling house in connection with the bombing of city detective Capt. Darrell Moody Feb. 16. Moody has been investigating the ring since nearly three years ago.

Taylor has been at large since the dynamiting.

Some of the evidence in the case may have been turned up in a search by FBI agents and state

police which drained a pond off Lovers Lane in May.

Several license plates from stolen cars were found in the mud of the pond when it was drained.

The grand jury charged one of the defendants, James Dennison of Bowling Green, and one of the conspirators, Barry Clayton, disposed of six license plates from stolen cars by throwing them into the pond in the fall and winter of 1970-71.

Three of the defendants, William Albert Hudson, Shirley Basham and James Hendricks, with conspirators Max Jacob Bayer and Melvin Eugene Moore, plotted to murder a potential witness, the indictment said. Hudson reportedly offered $3,000, later $5,000 for the murder, the indictment charged.

Basham said he would assist in the killing if necessary, and Hendricks reportedly traveled to Indianapolis to stress the importance of the killing with Bayer, the grand jury indictment said.

The indictment said a bomb was found under the car of the potential witness in Louisville on Jan. 21, 1971.

FBI officials refused to identify

Continued Back Page Column 2, This Section

ONE OF 23 PERSONS arrested Thursday in connection with a 10-state car theft ring, Larry Suddeth of Rt. 4, second from left, is...

Booke

Fifteen arrested in 10-state car theft ring

Bombing death of Hardin woman has police and friends asking why

Newspaper headline

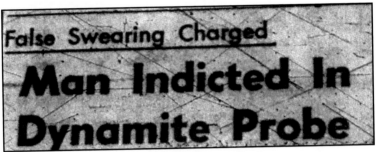

Man Indicted In Dynamite Probe

Grand Jury Hears Victim of Dynamiting Incidents

Father and Son Held to Grand Jury

Bomb Found Under Car of City Police Chief

Man Charged In Bombing Is Slain

Big Whiskey Still Hit By Police, Five Held In Adairville Raid

22/09/2017

A hearing for five men arrested in connection with a raid on a big moonshine still has been set for 10 a.m. Friday before U. S. District Court Commissioner Claudia Compton Bell.

The 2500-gallon capacity still was smashed Friday afternoon by Federal and State officers who had been hiding in a "stakeout" around the area since Wednesday.

The still was located near a tobacco patch 500 yards west of U.S. Hwy. 431 at the intersection of State Hwy. 663. This is about two miles north of Adairville and 10 miles south of Russellville.

Arrested and charged with operating the still were Carney Morgan Jr., 32; Arvil Knight, 53; and John Ewing Taylor, 44. Knight and Taylor are from Springfield, Tenn. Morgan lives and crops on the land for Henry Shoulders, 36, of Adairville, who in turn rents the place from Lou Byers of Bowling Green.

Shoulders and Clifton Gatewood, 54, also of Adairville, were cutting tobacco in a nearby field when the still was discovered. They were arrested but released on their own bond. They claimed they just happened to be working near the scene. The other three men were released after posting bonds of $1000 each.

Taylor and Knight were arrested at Adairville as they drove south toward Tennessee with what officers said was a load of illicit liquor from the still.

This was the largest still destroyed in Logan County in several years. After the news of the raid it was disclosed that another still was destroyed recently in the Lewisburg area, but there was no report of an arrest on this case.

Dynamite Find At Auburn Told To FBI

Logan County residents who watch Bowling Green's television station had to miss viewing over the weekend. The station, WLTV, was knocked off the air by dynamite.

The blast jarred WLTV's 601-foot high transmitting tower from its concrete base early Friday morning. It was thought to be the work of someone objecting to the station's free-wheeling commentary against crime and the conduct of local government. This was just conjecture, however, as there weren't many clues.

Over the weekend the FBI received a report from Ray Shaw, night policeman at Auburn, that he had stopped two men in a pickup truck Friday night who had five dynamite detonator caps and about 50 feet of fusing.

The men had committed no offense for which Shaw could hold them, he said, so he took their names and addresses and released them.

The shattered tower is located on U.S. Hwy. 231 13 miles northwest

Big Whiskey headline

Suspect In Bombing Jumps Bond

Billy B. Graham, 32, a former Edmonson Countian, indicted for the dynamiting last Oct. 15 of the Siddens Music Co., building, is the target of lawmen after jumping a Warren Circuit Court Bond.

* * *

Graham failed to appear before Circuit Judge John B. Rodes Friday and again yesterday. The $1,000 appearance bond was ordered forfeited and Rodes set a new bond for Graham at $2,500. Commonwealth Attorney Morris Lowe said he would have pressed for Graham's trial to be set tomorrow on the opening day of Allen Circuit Court at Scottsville if the defendant had appeared.

Reid Caudill, attorney for Graham, Friday withdrew a motion for change of venue in the case. The motion had not been ruled on.

Lowe's motion Friday that Graham's bond be forfeited after he failed to appear in court was overruled by Judge Rodes. The jurist said he would rule on the request for removal of the trial to Allen Circuit Court in Graham's presence on Saturday.

Guy McCormack is Graham's bondsman and has offered a reward of $100 for Graham's capture.

Lowe said Saturday every effort

Continued on page 4, column 3

Suspect in Bombing Jumps Bond

Sheriff Jim Johnson (left) escorts James Taylor Lovan to court during the Harper-Givens murder trial in Logan County, Kentucky.

Jim Johnson (center)

Jim Johnson

Jim Johnson (center)

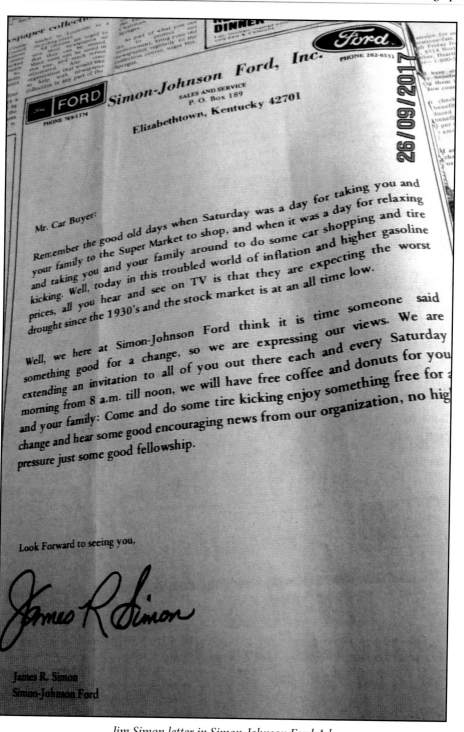

Jim Simon letter in Simon-Johnson Ford Ad

The Rhodes home on Youngers Creek Road as it looks today.

The Rhodes family barn in 2019 as it appears from the Bluegrass Parkway.

Johnson, when he traveled outside of Logan County, paid little attention to speed limits. If he was ever pulled over, he played his "state police" card. And it worked.

Even as a teenager growing up in Logan County, Johnson was known to enjoy trading cars, and now that he had done it in a big way, he had something else in mind. He wanted to be Logan County's next sheriff. But there was a problem and a big one. He was not Doc Beauchamp's chosen one. If he ran for the office, he had a big hill to climb.

Johnson put all of his eggs in one basket when Ford Motor Company informed him he couldn't own the dealership and be an elected official. He sold his interest to Harold Kitchens, Joe Dorris, and Ken Gilliam.

Jim Johnson was all in for sheriff.

He became the perfect candidate. His wife, Martha Ann, and their three boys were the ideal family. He was a member of the Masonic Lodge and the local Baptist church, a former state trooper, a Logan County native, a Navy veteran, and a member of the local American Legion Post.

At forty years old he campaigned on shutting down anything and everything illegal in the county, and the churches loved him. He even promised to solve one of the county's biggest mysteries: the murder of Lewisburg bank president Edgar Harper and his daughter Ella Givens, which occurred in 1965.

Six-day-long, sixty-hour weeks knocking on doors and shaking hands became the norm, but he could handle it. Young, energetic, fit, and personable, he was on a mission to become Sheriff of Logan County and, against all odds, he did.

Not only did Johnson win on May 27, 1969, but he was also the top vote-getter in the county. He was now thought to be the rising star in Logan County politics—the "white knight" who would follow Doc Beauchamp at the state level. That was tall cotton as Beauchamp had risen to Lt. Governor, State Treasurer, Senate Clerk, and a delegate to three Democratic National Conventions.

As the new sheriff Johnson had to prove he was all about law and order and that meant preventing local bootleggers from bringing in alcohol from nearby Bowling Green to his "dry" county.

By no means was Logan County the only adjacent county to Warren that had created their own cottage industry of legally buying liquor and beer and then re-selling it at marked-up prices in dry counties—Butler, Edmonson, Barren, Allen, Simpson, and even into Hart County and beyond. And it wasn't just John Bryant peddling the spirits in Bowling Green, either. There were a few others, but it was the Bryants who ruled.

The money that changed hands between bootleggers and their customers who purchased for convenience was major bucks. It was easy to see how important it was to Bowling Green liquor distributers to keep their paradise wet and all the other counties dry.

With Sheriff Johnson's apparent full-speed-ahead crackdown in Logan County, bootleggers had been warned. The county went dry in 1941, so bootleggers both black and white had a good run. However, in 1965, there had been enough local support from those who thought it was time for Logan County to sell booze legally. In spite of only getting on the ballot in March of that year, the drys won 1,485 to 877.

William "Botley" Todd, and his brother William Bennett Todd were two of the more well-known bootleggers in Russellville. Their Todd Cafe in the black section of town was a hot spot for purchasing spirits and finding an equally high-spirited gambling game. There were others: 5th Street Cafe, Lucie's, Francis Cafe, and Martin's Cafe in Adairville.

It was common knowledge that when election time rolled around, politicians knew if they had a chance of winning, they had to get out the black vote, and often it started with the black bootleggers.

Michael Morrow is a part of Russellville's Historic Russellville organization and his memories and research revealed that even though bootlegging and gambling was illegal, there was a certain amount of respect for them.

"Bootleggers here were a fairly close-knit group," Morrow said. "They'd get together annually to set the prices they would charge. So, at election time the questions they asked were 'How much you paying, and who will we vote for?'"

Sheriff Johnson knew who the players were, and periodically, his department would pull over suspected vehicles and confiscate their payload. It didn't take long before the Bowling Green suppliers sent word to Johnson that he could make all the stops he wanted to, but the alcohol belonged to them.

John Bryant and his son Jimmy were long considered the alcohol kingpins of south central Kentucky. Their Dixie Liquor store was a lucrative business, and their bottom line continued to grow as long as all of Warren County's surrounding counties remained dry. Whenever a rumor of a potential wet-dry vote raised its ugly head, the Bryants and everyone else who sold liquor and beer in Bowling Green became the biggest donors to all the opposition forces, which included mostly churches. The bootlegger trade was a huge business, and there were a certain few in Bowling Green who wanted to make sure it stayed that way. It was also important to note that even though Bowling Green was wet, the rest of Warren County was not.

Sheriff Johnson didn't take long before his department became known as "Johnson's Raiders." Bootleggers in Russellville and Logan County's other little towns of Olmstead, Lewisburg, Adairville and Auburn no longer had a safe haven. Residences suspected of stashing and selling beer and liquor were being put out of business. Johnson's department of deputies would coordinate with Kentucky State Police to be even more effective. Johnson, in full uniform, would accompany many of the raids. To further promote a campaign promise, the *Logan Leader* newspaper would be notified and be there on the raids to photograph the contraband seized. Of course, the pictures were published in the next edition. Johnson was fulfilling a campaign promise and shutting bootleggers down.

There were two raids, however, that drew more attention than usual and not necessarily in a good way.

On January 23, 1970, the Logan County Sheriff's Department and Kentucky State Police raided American Legion Post 29 in Russellville. In spite of Johnson's promises to rid the county of illegal alcohol, the Legion club felt it was "safe" because it was a private club. After all, six months earlier, Johnson and all his supporters celebrated his election victory there. Being a Navy veteran, he was a member and knew their playbook and what went on.

The raid netted almost $8,500 worth of illegal beverages, which included 8,634 cans of beer, and seven slot machines.

The Legion felt like they should have been off-limits for all it did for the city and county by way of sponsorships, involvement in charitable activities, and aiding destitute families of war veterans. That, the club thought, should have been enough to overlook a little drinking and gambling. They thought of themselves as untouchable.

The American Legion filed a suit claiming they had been illegally entered even though what they were doing was illegal. County Judge

Bob Brown fined Post 29 $63.50 for possession of alcohol and $213.50 for permitting gambling.

Next came a raid on the Russellville Country Club. No one was happy there either. But in both raids no one was arrested.

It was common knowledge that all the so-called private clubs in surrounding dry counties re-sold purchased alcohol from Bowling Green, and several of them even had slot machines like those at Legion Post 29 in Russellville. Most of the alcohol came from the Bryants, and guess where the slot machines came from?

A few years earlier in late January 1965, slot machines were found on College Street in Bowling Green in a building owned by John Bryant. He denied knowing anything about them and was not charged. Bryant did, however, plead guilty in police court to a charge of "breach of peace" after confronting a television news cameraman regarding the station's coverage of what the media thought to be a whole list of illegal doings in the area.

By now, everyone in Russellville and Logan County was well aware there was indeed a new sheriff in town.

CHAPTER FOURTEEN

Jim Johnson made a lot of campaign promises like most politicians do. Though voters might not have actually thought he would follow through with some of them, they were finding out he was.

He pledged to put more professionalism in the sheriff's department. His deputies were put in uniforms, utilized modern techniques, sent to police schools, was the first Logan County sheriff to appoint an African-American deputy, and worked tirelessly to solve crimes.

One of those crimes that had not been solved was the murder of eighty-one-year-old Edgar Casey Harper, and his forty-nine-year-old daughter, Ella Givens, on December 11, 1965, in Lewisburg, a few miles from Russellville. Harper was a former Lewisburg bank president and was thought to keep money at his home. It was a crime Johnson said would be a top priority for his department. True to his word, six months later three men were arrested for murder.

Logan County was ruled out for their trial because of the notoriety. Warren County was briefly considered but ruled out due to the corruptness at the time. Finally it was decided the three could get a fair trial in Christian County.

The suspects were tried individually, and when the first was found not guilty, Logan County prosecutors decided not to try the other two. It was a consensus among Logan County residents that justice had not prevailed, but Johnson had done all he could do.

Even though years earlier Johnson had said his only goal was to be the county sheriff, he began to set his political sights on becoming county judge.

The courthouse politicians hadn't taken him seriously before, and that proved to be a mistake. While campaigning for sheriff, he sold himself to the public as a "new face" and an experienced police officer who would, and did, professionalize the sheriff's office.

In his race for county judge, he would do as he had done in his sher-iff's race: heavy advertising, support of prominent citizens throughout the county, and, of course, at the top of the list were his accomplish-ments as sheriff.

Johnson's challenge to unseat County Judge Bob Brown was described in the local newspaper as a "tough, bruising contest." And when the dust settled in the 1973 May Democratic primary, Brown won. He had his contacts in Frankfort, and the fact that he was the state patronage leader in Logan County was too much for Johnson to overcome. As if a light switch had been turned off, Jim Johnson was out of a job. For now it ap-peared to him and his family that their future was not in Logan County.

He still had a bevy of contacts in Elizabethtown, or perhaps Bowling Green would be a good fit. He had a brother who was a vice president of one of the largest banks there, and that couldn't hurt. But he also knew that Warren County was going through a crime wave, and he wasn't sure that would be a good place for his family.

As Logan County's sheriff, he knew what all was going on in Bowl-ing Green, even to the point of knowing who the bad guys were. He didn't want to move there.

Perhaps returning to Elizabethtown would be the best choice. After spending almost seventeen years there with the Kentucky State Police, he had also enjoyed selling Fords for Dusty Rhodes part-time. From know-ing Rhodes like he did, he knew Dusty's dealership was always for sale.

Back to Elizabethtown he went. He knew Jim Simon, the sales man-ager at the dealership, and the two of them decided they would partner up and buy Dusty out.

Simon had been at the dealership for several years, learning the ropes and even acquiring stock in the business. He knew Jim Johnson, and with the contacts and outgoing personalities each had, there was no reason they couldn't make a go of it, in spite of rising interest rates and the potential for a military downsizing at nearby Ft. Knox with the Vietnam War drawing to a close.

Simon was an E-town guy. Having been a talented basketball and baseball player at Elizabethtown Catholic High School, he was well known. Following graduation in 1957, he had his sights set on college.

Simon enrolled at Bellarmine College in Louisville and enjoyed playing the ponies at nearby Churchill Downs. He had his wins, but like anybody who gambles, the losses usually override the wins.

One of those losses was in the fall of 1959. On his way to register for classes and pay tuition, he stopped off at the Downs with $800 cash in his pocket. Receiving a hot tip, he put it all on a horse to win. His bet lost by a nose at the wire, and with it, there went his college money.

In order to keep his mother and stepfather from finding out, he went to one of the automobile dealers in Elizabethtown, whose daughter Jim was dating at the time, and borrowed the money. He paid him back over time.

Simon proved he was a risktaker, so when Jim Johnson approached him about partnering up to buy Dusty Rhodes Ford, he agreed. Johnson had inherited a little money, and what better place to put it than into his future.

In September 1973, Dusty Rhodes Ford became Simon-Johnson Ford.

It didn't take long for all the parties—Rhodes, Simon, and Johnson—to realize the business was like quicksand, and they were sinking fast.

By late July 1974, the nation's prime rate began to spike upward to 9 percent, 10 percent, 11 percent, and 12 percent. It was becoming unprofitable for banks to make car loans. New car loans were at 10.2 percent, while used cars ranged from 11.5 percent to over 12 percent, depending on the vehicle's age. Loans, however, were still being made because of competition between banks.

Car dealers were paying more for the cost of "floor planning" than the customer was paying for a loan to buy the car. Floor planning is a system in which the car dealer purchases cars from the factory to display on their lot and showroom and takes orders. These cars had to be paid for in advance, and the majority of dealers had to borrow money to purchase them. In 1974, dealers were paying at least 12 percent since "floor planning" was traditionally tied to the prime rate.

Dealers across the country had difficulty keeping a large inventory on their lots for thirty to sixty days like they did when rates were lower. New Fords were selling for around $4,000, but yearly inflation was a choking 11.3 percent. Gas was averaging 55¢ a gallon, but still there was talk of a gasoline shortage. And if the economy wasn't bad enough, the country was embroiled in the Watergate scandal, which led to President Richard Nixon's resignation on August 9, 1974.

It was not a good time to be in the automobile business.

Even though Rhodes had technically sold his dealership to Simon and Johnson, he was still a part of the business because he hadn't been paid in full.

All along while he was working as sales manager, Simon had been buying stock from Rhodes in the Ford dealership and owned enough that he didn't have to put any money in the purchase transaction.

Johnson, on the other hand, had to buy a new stock issue, and the corporation had to buy up shares of stock that Rhodes controlled as president of the corporation. The money owed to Rhodes was $180,000.

Rhodes turned around and purchased back the Ford Tractor portion of the business from the corporation, reducing the amount owed to him to $128,500.

The three—Rhodes, Simon and Johnson—entered into a security agreement that said the corporation would maintain an insurance policy on Rhodes' life for the amount of the note, with his wife named beneficiary.

The $128,500 that Simon and Johnson owed Rhodes was set up on monthly payments of $1,500 plus 8.5 percent interest.

Simon-Johnson Ford was in trouble. Undercapitalized and owing not only $128,500 to Rhodes but also $250,000 to Citizens Bank in Elizabethtown and $100,000 to Ford Motor Credit Corporation for cars they had already sold without paying for them, the pressure was on.

Rhodes went to them and asked to get back in the dealership.

"The place was getting into trouble," he said. "I wanted them to let me into the deal to see what could be done to salvage it."

Rhodes went back several times to talk about the situation. Johnson and Rhodes got into an argument. Rhodes told Johnson that he was "too stupid and ignorant to talk about it."

For good reason that made Johnson mad, and he quickly left the room and then later stuck his head back into the doorway, saying, "I'll show you how ignorant I am."

Rhodes then told Simon that he "better get Johnson to listen to us, or they're going to close the dealership down in a week."

CHAPTER FIFTEEN

D usty Rhodes felt like he was protected financially when it came to his wife, Peggy. He had three life insurance policies assigned to Citizens Bank to secure a small business loan. This loan was a corporation indebtedness that Simon and Johnson had assumed, paying the premiums on these policies on Rhodes' life worth about $150,000. According to the purchase agreement, the benefits would go to the agency if Rhodes died. The dealership would have paid off the remaining debt to Peggy Rhodes.

The three policies assigned to Citizens Bank were to be replaced by policies on the lives of Simon and Johnson, and the beneficiary on Rhodes' policies were to be changed to Peggy. It never happened.

Jack Scott, president of Citizens Bank, had pretty much handled the Dusty Rhodes Ford account himself, but finally he decided to turn some of the grunt work that required lots of attention to James Payton, one of the bank's loan officers.

Several people in the know saw the car dealership as a failing business, heavily in debt.

One of those was Alma Williams, the bookkeeper for the business. She had worked for Dusty a number of years and continued with Simon and Johnson when they took over the agency.

"There wasn't any money when I started working, and there wasn't any money when it closed," she said.

Jim Simon, in his own words, said the dealership was not financially sound since the day Rhodes opened it. He said the firm's financial statement was inaccurate from the beginning and that it never was corrected.

Still, over the next few years, Simon bought stock in the dealership, and by the time Rhodes cut himself out of the business in 1973, Jim Simon owned 51 percent of the stock.

The relationship between Jim Johnson and Rhodes had become out-wardly strained, and taking it further, both Simon and Johnson thought Rhodes had misrepresented the dealership when he sold it to them.

A former Elizabethtown banker not involved in the business trans-actions of the Ford dealership recalled that he and several others felt like Rhodes had sold Simon and Johnson a "pig-in-a-poke." "But they should have known," he said.

In early December 1974, Johnson and Simon met with County At-torney James Scudder to determine whether they had been criminally swindled by Rhodes. At one point in the meeting, Simon pointed his finger and said, "We may not be able to get him in court, but I'll tell you one thing, he has screwed us for the last time he's going to screw anybody, even if I have to go out there and take it out of his hide."

Simon later said his statement was, "The only thing we can get out of Dusty would be out of his hide."

He said he was only trying to talk Johnson out of suing Rhodes because he knew Rhodes was in as bad of financial condition as "we were in."

Scudder, the County Attorney, said he never heard Simon make such a statement about Rhodes, but he did recall sometime in late No-vember or early December 1974, Jim Johnson coming to his office and closing the door behind him.

"He didn't say a thing," Scudder said. "He had his pipe in his mouth. He sat down, took the pipe out of his mouth, looked at me, and said, 'I believe before I can die happy, I'm going to have to kill the s.o.b.' He put his pipe in his mouth and walked out."

Payton, the bank officer, said he too heard Johnson threaten to kill Rhodes but never heard Simon make a threat. Payton added that John-son said he was going to "kill that s.o.b. or have it done."

Johnson had been described by those who knew him in Elizabeth-town and Russellville as flamboyant and something of a likable brag-gart who, on more than one occasion, boasted of having underworld connections left over from his law enforcement days.

"He once said he could have somebody blown away for a hundred bucks," an Elizabethtown acquaintance told the *Louisville Times*. "And he said it in such a way that you never knew if he was kidding or not."

The Kentucky State Police didn't put much stock in Johnson's com-ments. After all, he had been one of them for years, and they knew how he was.

"Ah, for those of us who knew Johnson well, and we've known him all his life, we know that he is kind of a flighty person who is just a big talker," offered one of his trooper buddies.

Johnson learned to fly an airplane when he was with the Kentucky State Police and came close to getting fired when he flew under the Clark Memorial Bridge over the Ohio River in Louisville. Someone got the number of his plane, which led to serious trouble with the state.

With financial desperation becoming more real every day, friends in Elizabethtown and Logan County advised Johnson to look into bankruptcy. By all accounts he had taken out another mortgage on his home, and he reasoned there were still other ways to save the Ford dealership.

Jim Simon was equally feeling the pressure. He was advised to cut expenses. He asked bookkeeper Alma Williams to contact Home Insurance Company to see the amount of money the dealership was paying for life insurance, whom the beneficiary would be, and for how much.

He was looking at every angle to cut expenses, as each day the business was falling further behind. Citizens Bank, Ford Motor Credit, and Ford Motor Company were the main obligations they had, but equally important was that they had a payroll to meet.

Pressure, especially financial pressure, will make a person act and do things far out of the ordinary. It's a heavy burden to bear, especially when family and community status is involved. To fold up Simon-Johnson Ford would have been an embarrassment and, to a point, humiliating.

Jim Simon and Jim Johnson had led trustworthy lives. Simon had been the always-smiling star athlete who dated all the pretty girls, married a local beauty, and made something of himself as a successful car salesman.

Johnson had served in the Navy and been a highly respected state trooper and the sheriff of Logan County, where he was a strict law-and-order man.

And now all of this was crumbling down right in front of their eyes. Everything they had been taught by their mamas and daddies, everything they had taken away from the years of church sermons they had heard, all of the little stories they had told to their young children in hopes of directing them to the "right things to do" in life: Be truthful. Lead an honorable life.

All of this was about to be put to the test.

CHAPTER SIXTEEN

The new Ford sped south down I-65. In it Jim Johnson was driving, and Jim Simon was in the passenger seat. They were headed to Cave City, where Johnson and Simon were to meet an acquaintance of Johnson's at Jerry's Restaurant, just off the interstate at Exit 53. It was Simon's impression he was going to appraise a car that belonged to David Cooper Walker.

Supposedly Walker and Johnson had developed a "warm friendship" in June 1974, when Walker stopped by the Simon-Johnson dealership to talk about trading cars. They even talked about going into some kind of business together.

With Johnson's law enforcement background and Walker's history of always running from the law, it would seem the only thing they had in common was both having been in the Navy. But perhaps they might enter into business together after all. It seemed odd.

Walker had gotten a phone call to his unlisted number from Johnson the morning of December 1, asking if he could meet him somewhere that afternoon. When Walker said he already had something to do, the two agreed on the following day for lunch at the Cave City Jerry's.

Arriving at the crowded restaurant, the three shook hands and were escorted to a table. It didn't take long for Johnson to explain to Walker the reason he had phoned him.

Walker said both Johnson and Simon told him they had a job for him … needed to have someone taken care of.

"Are you talking about having someone killed?" Walker asked. "Yes," they answered.

Was this the business Walker and Johnson were talking about back in June?

Walker told the two a crowded restaurant was not the place to talk about having someone killed and suggested they go outside.

They finished their lunch and walked out to the parking lot. Johnson had already told Walker the relationship he and Dusty Rhodes had. He said Rhodes had beaten him out of a large sum of money when he first bought into the dealership and that Rhodes was on the verge of hurting both Simon and Johnson financially. They needed Rhodes taken care of.

Making sure no one else was in earshot, Walker told Johnson he could take care of their problem for $10,000 cash and a new Thunderbird. "Too high," Johnson fired back.

Walker didn't blink on his fee, and he headed back to Bowling Green and Johnson and Simon to Elizabethtown.

All three had a lot to think about.

The financial crisis for both Jim Johnson and Jim Simon was becoming more desperate with each passing day. A couple of days passed before Johnson called Walker and said they had a deal.

Walker could probably have said $20,000 and a new T-bird, and they would have been all in. No matter what the price, money was going to have to be borrowed to pay Walker. They would have to figure out later how to cover the $7,700 cost of the new Thunderbird. They would deal with Ford Motor Credit on that. Their main concern for the moment was getting Dusty Rhodes off their books. The $150,000 in life insurance policies on him would help relieve some of the financial stress ... for the time being.

Although David Walker had received no down payment to eliminate Rhodes, he went ahead and contacted Steve Monroe in Bowling Green, who he knew could get the job done. Monroe agreed to do the job for $5,000.

The date Walker reached his verbal agreement with Johnson and Simon coincided with the mid-December 1974 rental of Neal Turner's house and garage in Bowling Green by Carlos Lloyd.

"I rode with Steve ... took me to David Walker's house," Lloyd said. "At first I didn't know why. Then he told me Walker wanted someone to kill a Mr. Rhodes in E-town. He said we'd split $10,000. He said the money was to come from two guys there. All Walker wanted out of it was a new car. He was giving Monroe and me the money."

Lloyd said he waited outside while Steve went inside and came back with $500 for each of them as a down payment (Walker later testified he only gave Monroe $500 total). The two then drove to Walmart, where Monroe went in and bought a fishing tackle box with a handle. It was one without a tray inside.

"We had ten sticks of dynamite that Steve had been stealing and hidden in his dad's attic," Lloyd continued. "It was at the farmhouse where we assembled the bomb. We took a piece of plywood board, a triggering device, 6-volt battery, used a plastic spoon handle to separate the connecting points, and taped it up."

David Walker returned to the Simon-Johnson Ford dealership in E-town soon after the meeting at Jerry's Restaurant to make sure he knew where Dusty Rhodes lived. He needed a map on how to get there, and Jim Simon, Walker said, was the one who drew it up because Johnson was too nervous.

While everyone, including investigators, thought the bomb at Rhodes' farm had been placed on January 12 or 13 of 1975, Lloyd had a completely different story. And it was a shocker.

"It was about the first of January. We drove my $200 1967 Buick LeSabre up to Mr. Rhodes' place just off the Bluegrass Parkway. I parked it on the parkway and raised the hood. Steve was carrying the bomb. We had to climb over two fences. One of them was barbed wire. I stood at the corner of the barn, watching the house. It was probably close to midnight, but it took a pretty good while, maybe fifteen minutes for Steve to place the bomb."

Lloyd offered that he and Monroe never thought about getting caught. After all it was midnight and who would be up then, except bad guys doing bad things? New Year's Eve had come and gone, and now most normal people needed their rest.

"If anyone had spotted us, we would have run," said Lloyd. "We didn't have guns with us, and if the bomb had gone off, it would have killed Steve, and I could probably get back to the car and gotten away."

If, in fact, the bomb had been set some two weeks before it exploded, how was it not set off earlier by Peggy or the neighbor feeding Tony? Didn't anyone ever feed the horse? Didn't they go in the feed room? It didn't make sense, but it was Carlos Lloyd's story, and no one was around to refute it.

The timeline Lloyd presented made sense … well sort of. The timing on the rental farmhouse fit with their agreement with Walker. So, by the time they drove from Bowling Green to Youngers Creek Road to scout things out, it was the last week in December 1974.

"Steve told me Walker said they didn't have a dog," Carlos Lloyd said. "So, there wouldn't be a barking dog. If they had one, Walker may have gotten rid of it ... we didn't."

Monroe and Lloyd had also been told Dusty Rhodes went to the barn every day to feed the horse.

No one will ever know what happened to the two dogs on the Rhodes' farm. Maybe they did run away. Or maybe Walker did eliminate them. Or perhaps Steve Monroe and Carlos Lloyd were so efficient and quiet that night that they let sleeping dogs lie.

"It was Steve's idea to use the bomb," Lloyd said. "It was his M.O. (mode of operation). After it was set I actually thought about going back to the barn to get the bomb. After thinking about all the time that had passed since we placed it, maybe Steve didn't really set it but was instead just testing me to see how far I would go with him."

Steve Monroe and Carlos Lloyd weren't the only ones wondering why they had not heard about Dusty Rhodes' death. David Walker was getting phone calls from Jim Johnson in Elizabethtown.

"From the time I hired Monroe until the bomb went off about a month later, both Simon and Johnson pressured me to have the job done immediately," said Walker.

He in turn contacted Monroe, telling him the people in Elizabethtown were unhappy because the elimination had not occurred. Monroe assured Walker that it would happen. Monroe and Lloyd talked every day after setting the bomb. Why hadn't it gone off? Don't they ever feed the horse? One week went by and then another. What they didn't realize was that Monroe had set the explosive connected to the tack room door and not the feed stall.

A few days later Simon and Johnson were on their way to Elkton, Kentucky for some business and wanted to meet with Walker in Bowling Green. He agreed and met them in the bar at the Ramada Inn, just off I-65. They again told him they were "deeply concerned about the time element." They were unaware at this point that it was a bomb that was to kill Dusty Rhodes.

"It could happen any time," Walker assured them, even suggesting they get back to Elizabethtown so they would be visible when it happened.

Walker contacted Steve Monroe again, and Monroe told him that the job was "75 per cent complete." It was then that Monroe told him about the bomb he and Lloyd had planted in the barn.

Walker said he thought planting a bomb was a "damn fool thing" and insisted Monroe remove it. He refused.

Walker, after learning about the bomb, said he warned Johnson and Simon that the bomb had been planted in the Rhodes' barn and that two or three people could be killed by such an explosion. Their reaction was mild, according to Walker's trial testimony, and one of them expressed the hope that the "old man who feeds the horses isn't one of them."

Monroe later said Walker knew all along that he planned to kill Dusty Rhodes with a bomb. Walker had thought that Monroe and Lloyd would take out the Elizabethtown car dealer with a high-powered rifle bullet from the nearby tree line.

Walker had visited Simon-Johnson Ford in Elizabethtown on several occasions, but when he returned on January 15, 1975, he learned that the bomb Steve Monroe and Carlos Lloyd had set had finally exploded.

CHAPTER SEVENTEEN

P eggy Rhodes had walked into her horse barn on Youngers Creek Road on a frigid late afternoon on January 13, 1975. The last words that probably came out of her mouth were "Binky, Binky." She was looking for her cat, and it could be anywhere in the barn.

The initiating fire train for the device, with the exception of the electric blasting cap, was mounted on a length of common 1 x 4 board about seven or eight inches long. A 6-volt dry cell battery was affixed to the length of board with several wraps of black plastic tape. A set of Briggs and Stratton engine ignition points were used to create an electrical circuit booby trap. The ignition points were adjusted so that they were in a closed position—in other words, making contact. A small plastic spoon handle was placed between the closed ignition points, causing the electrical circuit to be held in the open position. A length of fishing line was attached to the plastic spoon. Wire leads from the negative and positive poles of the battery were attached to each side of the ignition points, and the same was done with the electric blasting cap leg wires. Eight pounds of 1 1/4 inch by 8 inch dynamite was then placed inside of a metal fishing tackle box, which was approximately 12 inches long by 7 inches wide by 6 inches deep. The tackle box had an aluminum, hang type carry handle on top. The length of board holding the battery and ignition points was affixed to the bottom of the tackle box by black electrical tape. An electric blasting cap was seated in one of the sticks of high explosives. The improvised explosive device (IED) was hung by a large nail on the inside of the door to the horse barn tack room at about chest height. The trip attached to the plastic spoon handle was then attached to the door frame. The bomb was set and operational.

When Peggy Rhodes swung open the tack room door, the trip wire caused the plastic spoon handle to be pulled from between the ignition points, instantly closing an electrical circuit. The completed circuit caused the blasting cap to explode and initiate the high explosives. The explosive used was Austin Powder Company 60% dynamite, which produces a detonation velocity of 12,000 to 15,000 feet per second. (The above description of the bomb set up was given by ATF Special Agent Bill Rockliff.)

Peggy and her horse Tony never saw a thing, never heard a sound, and never felt any pain. That was the only good in this horrific explosion.

To reconstruct such a crime scene takes years of experience. ATF Laboratory Analyst Charlie Connor deserved much of the credit for determining how the device was constructed. He took what ATF agents and Kentucky State Police had collected while crawling around the barn's dirt floor, literally sifting through the debris looking for evidence left from the explosion. One of those pieces of evidence was found on the underside of a piece of black electrical tape. Connor discovered a nearly complete index fingerprint.

The evidence that ATF Agent Bill Rockliff had personally driven to Cincinnati's ATF Laboratory now came full circle with the fingerprint.

Special Agent Connor had been with the agency since 1955 and, before that, with the Indiana State Police. He attended and studied fingerprinting in virtually every fingerprinting school in the country. His workplace was no more than a small lab in the Federal Office Building in Cincinnati. He went about his job operating fuming cabinets, exhaust hoods, various types of magnifiers, and an assortment of light sources. All were part of determining whether a fingerprint could eliminate or convict a crime suspect. He was so good at what he did that he testified more than 200 times as an expert witness across the United States.

Fingerprints are a person's identification in that it is the recording of the tip end of an individual's finger that is individual to itself. The probability of two fingerprints being alike from different fingers is one to the tenth to the fortieth power, which has been estimated to be twenty times more than the estimated population of the world.

Normally, for Agent Connor, he used twelve key points of a fingerprint in identifying it. However, for this particular fingerprint found on the sticky side of the black tape at the barn where Peggy Rhodes died, he found fourteen points.

Fingerprinting has long been used in crimes, also in identifying accident victims, and even as a security source for opening and closing doors. But with every "punch," there is often a "counter punch" that can mess up a good thing. So, surely a fingerprint could be forged or planted without a person's knowledge.

"I've attempted several times to pick my own print and put it someplace else by lifting it on adhesive tape or trying to move it around and place it someplace else," Agent Connor said. "I have not been able to do that, and no reports have ever been confirmed that it is possible to place an image of a known print someplace else other than by the individual who has it."

A fingerprint had been lifted from the Park City Mobile Home sales office bombing back in May 1974 in Bowling Green that eventually led to the arrest of Steve Monroe.

"In the business we were in, bartenders, barmaids, beauticians, and barbers were some of our best sources," said ATF Agent Bob Bridgewater. "I got very little information from church people."

Agent Bridgewater had lots of contacts in Bowling Green's underworld.

"I had an informant in the car theft ring that told me Monroe, Lloyd, and Walker were up to something in Elizabethtown," recalled Bridgewater. "Bill Haverstick was an ATF agent here in Bowling Green, and Monroe's name kept coming up on the Park City Mobile Home bombing. We arrested him and took his fingerprints."

Out on bail and probably going to get off with little more than a slap on the wrist, Monroe had yet to be brought to trial. But like many criminals, he couldn't resist the temptation of easy money and a self-confidence of being able to flaunt his criminal activities in the face of the law.

With no particular known motive for anyone to kill Peggy Rhodes, ATF and Kentucky State Police quickly theorized she probably wasn't the intended victim. The investigation turned up some leads, but nothing credible.

"We had a meeting in Louisville to see if we had a federal case," said Bridgewater. "It was close to being dropped. I met with Special Agents Dick Johnston and Dick Guernsey, who was in charge of the Louisville office, and they asked me what I thought, and I said yes, I think we have something."

And then on March 27, 1975, more than two months after the Youngers Creek Road bombing, an arrest was made in Bowling Green. Steve Leo Monroe, twenty-four, was apprehended by ATF agents Dick Johnston, Frank Guernsey, Bob Bridgewater, and State Police Detective Walter Sims, at his home in Bowling Green. It was the second time in a year that Monroe had been taken in by the ATF.

"At approximately 7 a.m., I executed a federal arrest warrant for Steve Leo Monroe at his residence in Warren County," said Agent Johnston. "I advised him of his rights to remain silent, his rights to have an attorney. He stated that he understood his rights."

Johnston then asked permission to search Monroe's residence. Monroe granted the agents permission for the search, which turned up a vial of liquid that proved to be mercury, which was sometime used in bomb making with a timing apparatus. Also found was a roll of Scotch brand black electrical tape.

Monroe was immediately taken to Louisville, where he was arraigned before U.S. Magistrate Dale Booth. He was charged with making and possessing a destructive device that killed Mrs. Paul F. Rhodes. Hardin County Commonwealth Attorney Hobson James said he might also seek additional indictments.

The following day, State Police Lt. Walter Sims told the media that Monroe was a native of Colorado and had no connection with Peggy Rhodes nor had he ever lived in Hardin County. Sims also said the bomb Monroe was accused of assembling was made of commercial dynamite, packed in a metal container and rigged to a homemade detonator and trip wire. Earlier, soon after the bombing death, Sims had said it was TNT that caused the explosion.

"What was the motive?", Sims was asked. "The motive question is still under investigation," he said.

Sims provided a timeline, saying the bomb was installed between 10 a.m., January 12, and the time of the explosion at approximately 5 p.m., January 13. He concluded by saying the investigation was being conducted by the Kentucky State Police, Hardin County Sheriff's Office, and ATF.

The case was to go to the May term of the U.S. grand jury in Louisville. Monroe would be held at the Jefferson County Jail in federal custody in lieu of a $100,000 bond.

On April 16, 1975, Bridgewater visited Monroe at the Jefferson County Jail after receiving a letter from him the previous day. Monroe had been arrested the month before, and as he sat in jail, not sure of what was happening on the outside, he wrote Agent Bridgewater:

Bob, I'm writing because I didn't know what to do and I thought you might be able to help me. First of all, my wife hasn't got any money at all. She is in her second year at Western, and I've done all a man could do to keep her in school, I am flat broke. She needs some help. She graduated from Warren Central as valedictorian and was granted two scholarships, but she got pregnant and lost both of them. She's making straight A's in college. I don't want to see her drop out. Is there anything I can do?

Second, is my ex-wife is depending on my child support and she needs the money pretty bad, too. She has to have the money to even make ends meet. I haven't seen my lawyer, but two times since I've been here. My dad is worse off than any of us. I sure would thank you a whole lot if you could help, Bob. Steve L. Monroe.

On the back of the letter he wrote how both his wife and ex-wife could be contacted and then added, "I know neither have a dime to their name, and both have one of my children."

Agent Bridgewater had a thirty-minute conversation with Monroe that involved Monroe saying he wanted to go back into business with his father. He was asking about financial aid for his wife and ex-wife.

"I told him there was probably some state aid or welfare for his present family," said Bridgewater. "But I doubted whether any would cover his ex-family."

Bridgewater said Monroe became very emotional, even crying, and dropped his head like he was in a state of concern, while asking, "Why did that woman go to the barn?"

Later Monroe denied asking Bridgewater that question.

Monroe went to trial on May 29, 1975, proclaiming his complete innocence on anything and everything, and a court-appointed attorney, Robert E. Fleming, was assigned to him. Twenty-eight-year-old Steve Pitt, Assistant U.S. Attorney, would handle the prosecution for the government. He had been with the Department of Justice since 1972, specializing in criminal trial work, and was Chief of the Criminal Division since 1974.

Fleming was a Louisville criminal lawyer who had represented one of the two Tinsley brothers who fatally shot two Louisville policemen in May 1971. Later he represented former Kentucky School Superintendent Alice McDonald in a theft of service trial.

Fleming ranked first in his graduating class at the University of Louisville in 1959. He had been a Quarterly Court Judge and the assistant prosecutor for the Commonwealth of Kentucky, a job he resigned in 1971, at the age of thirty-nine. He was making $7,000 a year.

(Several years later Fleming represented Gary "Tank" Allen of *Cornbread Mafia* notoriety. Though the book says Allen was convicted, Fleming says his client, Allen, was acquitted.)

In the very beginning of the pre-trial process, Monroe was charged with the murder of Peggy Rhodes. Robert Fleming, his attorney, never wanted the case to go to federal court. Fleming felt that defending Monroe would be more successful if done in state court.

"No attorney wanted to touch this case," recalled Fleming years later. "Thinking it would be tried in Hardin County, it was thought Monroe could not get a fair trial."

The trial was taking place in front of Judge Rhodes Bratcher in U.S. District Court. He had been appointed to his judgeship by President Richard Nixon in 1970, and at fifty-seven years old, he had a facial resemblance to President Lyndon Johnson.

Bratcher's wily, folksy, country-spin manner could often be disarming to both prosecutors and defense because he quickly earned a reputation of speaking to the point. (He died of a heart attack at the age of fifty-nine in 1977.) The jurors seemed to like him, too.

"I don't know how difficult it is for you to get lunch around this area," he told them. "I'm not talking about a good lunch. I know how difficult it is to get a good lunch anytime ... but, just to get a lunch that you will be able to survive on."

The trial consisted of six counts against Monroe:

- Count one, he did unlawfully make a destructive device;
- Count two, he did unlawfully possess a destructive device;
- Count three, he did maliciously damage by means of exploding a building and personal property used in and affecting interstate commerce, the office of Park City Mobile Homes;
- Count four, on or about January 13, 1975, unlawfully made a destructive device;

- Count five, on or about January 13, 1975, did unlawfully possess a destructive device;
- Count six, on or about January 13, 1975, he did maliciously damage, by means of explosives, a building and personal property used in and affecting interstate commerce, and in doing so did cause the death of Mrs. Paul F. Rhodes.

In a creative way, Assistant U.S. Attorney Steve Pitt, tied the death of Peggy Rhodes to her horse Tony and the impact the horse had on interstate commerce.

Fleming never forgot how a federal case was made out of the murder.

CHAPTER EIGHTEEN

A federal case was indeed made out of the Peggy Rhodes murder. In past years it seemed like the FBI took credit for most of the big cases, and in the eyes of ATF agents across the country, it was always "The FBI announced the arrest of...."

But now the ATF was finally getting their dues in a federal case.

The Kentucky State Police and ATF did much of the groundwork, and it had only been lately that the ATF became more visible about what they did. The agency's policy was to stay out of the limelight, thus making their efforts more effective.

Assistant U. S. Attorney Steve Pitt tied the death of Peggy Rhodes and her horse Tony to interstate commerce, and the bombing in Bowling Green at Park City Mobile Home Sales fit the same criteria.

"The horse that died had been used to herd and roundup cattle," Fleming said. "Then they were sold across state lines. That was the connection."

The feds and state police also searched the property in Bowling Green that Carlos Lloyd had leased from Neal Turner, a realtor.

It was the first time Lloyd's name had been introduced pertaining to the murder of Peggy Rhodes.

Both Judge Bratcher and Fleming, Steve Monroe's attorney, wondered who was this Lloyd guy and what did he have to do with the case.

"It eludes me at this point," Bratcher told the jury.

But now, for the first time, Steve Monroe and Carlos Lloyd had been connected.

By February 16, 1975, Lloyd and Monroe had vacated the Neal Turner property they had first rented on December 16, 1974.

The pair was there long enough to chop up a few stolen cars before assembling a bomb. It would be a bomb that would ultimately change the lives of several families in Bowling Green and Elizabethtown.

Gary Lusher was one of those in charge of special investigations for the Kentucky State Police, and he was following a lead that wound up at the property rented by Carlos Lloyd on 31-W.

"I went out to that farm investigating some stolen pickup trucks," Lusher recalled. "We got a search warrant, but by then, Lloyd and Monroe had already left."

ATF Agent Bob Bridgewater was also involved in the search on March 6, 1975, and what the two of them would find turned out to be major incriminating evidence in solving the Peggy Rhodes' murder.

"There was evidence who had lived there had been doing some grinding (on cars)," said Lusher. "But it was apparent they were doing some other stuff, as well."

And, indeed they were.

"There was a large tree stump on the property that had a house built around it," Agent Bridgewater said. "It was what they used as a work bench."

The tree stump was crucial evidence as it was chemically tested for anything that could be used in assembling a bomb. It did. But to further add to building a case against Monroe and Lloyd, an invoice with Monroe's name on it was found. It was from a local hardware store, and the item on it was roofing nails, the same kind used in the bomb that killed Peggy Rhodes.

Years later Gary Lusher remembered Steve Monroe well. "He was a big punk. When he was a young teenager, he was always in small trouble. I pulled him over a few times because of the way he drove. I remember one time I told him if he kept it up, he was headed for big trouble. And he was."

It was in Monroe's early years that a young Bowling Green attorney, not long out of law school, was hired to represent him. "He shot and killed a farmer's duck. He said he did it because he had never eaten duck and wanted to try it," the attorney explained. "That might have been a sign of things to come."

As the federal trial against Monroe progressed, Assistant U.S. Attorney Steve Pitt called three fingerprint experts in their attempt to connect Monroe directly to the bomb.

"I cross-examined the first two and felt pretty good," Monroe's attorney Fleming remembers. "But the clincher against Monroe was that third witness. He took a piece of black electrical tape found at the crime scene, peeled back the sticky part, and showed a fingerprint in a blown-up photo. It was so good it looked like the print had been taken right there in the courtroom. I knew we were in trouble from that print. It was not good either when I heard one of the jurors say, 'That's amazing' when he saw the print. Fleming, in a bit of creative lawyering himself, did his best to get all the fingerprint testimony from ATF Agent Connor suppressed. He based his motion on the arrest and fingerprinting of Steve Monroe in March 1975.

Fleming told Judge Rhodes Bratcher and the court that his client was arrested solely on the fingerprint evidence. He then went on to say that the actual positive identification of the print belonging to Monroe didn't happen until after his arrest.

Fleming's effort to suppress the fingerprint testing was overruled.

Jimmy Brown, Ron "Stormy" Stronk, and Ronnie Klokoc all testified against Monroe. Fleming tried to discredit Brown's testimony that he had given at a February hearing where he said he did the bombing, not Monroe. But now Brown was saying he lied then because of a threat made on his wife's life.

Brown's criminal history was such that it was easy to persuade him to speak out against his old teenage buddy, Steve Monroe. Not only did he help Monroe make the bomb that blew up the Park City Mobile Home Sales Office, but Brown was also connected to three murders in Michigan.

These were characters, not out of Disney World, but Bowling Green, Kentucky.

Brown had been a mechanic at Yellow Cab Company in Bowling Green, and according to ATF Agent Bridgewater, he was involved in everything bad.

"Brown is the one who told me about Monroe's method of making bombs ... tape covered by paint," said Bridgewater. "Frank Guernsey and I went to Michigan to interview him in prison. He told us everything about Monroe. I asked if there was anything I could do for him. He said, 'Yes.' From his window he could see the tip top of a McDonald's sign. He told us he wanted a triple-pounder, fries, and a Coke. We were able to get it for him."

Bridgewater went on to say Brown did his time, came back to Bowling Green, straightened his life out, married for a while, and then divorced. Later he committed suicide.

Monroe himself testified and denied virtually every point of the government's case against him. He said he had nothing to do with the bombing in Bowling Green or the bombing that had killed Peggy Rhodes. He said all the thirty-five witnesses against him were lying, and "to my knowledge, that's not my fingerprint."

Judge Bratcher was ready to bring this murder trial to an end.

Monroe's lawyer, Fleming, said in closing, "You know, there's an old saying in boxing. 'If you don't have a punch, you dazzle 'em with your footwork.' And I submit to you that's what the government has tried to do here. Bring in all this stuff, get you all confused thinking about all these wonderful scientific tests they've done, when all they've got is one fingerprint."

Judge Bratcher gave each attorney thirty minutes for closing arguments, but when he called out "five minutes," Fleming went at least another fifteen.

It was Pitt's turn:

"In every case that comes down the pike, the defense attorney is going to say to you that it's the most ridiculous case he's ever seen, and it's the worst case he's ever seen. That's lawyer talk."

Pitt continued, "The United States (prosecution) brought in some punks. I said they weren't angels. Maybe they are punks. In my experience angels run around with and fly around angels, and punks run around with punks."

He went on to point out that the Park City Mobile Home Sales office and the Rhodes' farm were heavily engaged in interstate commerce, and that's where we get the federal jurisdiction in this case.

Pitt reminded the jury to remember Steve Monroe's demeanor during the trial. His complete denial of everything presented as evidence that tied him to the two crimes. In his short time on the witness stand, he exhibited a brash sort of arrogant attitude, Pitt said.

Steve Pitt, loud and clear, made sure the jury remembered the four fingerprint experts had found Steve Leo Monroe's fingerprint connected to both the Park City Mobile Home and Peggy Rhodes bombings.

The government said Monroe had the knowledge and access to explosives and that he had the tendency to make bombs.

At no time in the trial was Steve Monroe's Marine Corps service mentioned, mainly because attorney Robert Fleming was unaware of it and for good reason. It was not something Monroe talked about other than to his friends. His less than honorable discharge would have not served him well in front of the jury.

"I had no idea he was ever in the Marines," Fleming said later. "If it had been one of honor, I would have certainly brought it up.

After the two-and-a-half day trial, the case was given to the jury.

Assistant U.S. Attorney Steve Pitt called thirty-seven witnesses and Monroe's attorney Robert Fleming only took two hours to present his defense. Nowhere in any of the testimony did the trial answer why a bomb was placed on the Rhodes' farm and who had ordered the bombing.

The jury was out only forty-five minutes before federal marshals called the attorneys back into the courtroom.

"The jury's back?" Fleming asked. The marshal nodded. Fleming, who had been talking to reporters, looked at them and bit his lower lip.

"Uh, okay, that's too quick. Something's wrong," he said.

"Guilty on all six counts that included life imprisonment on count six," read the jury's foreman, Freddie Gee.

Steve Monroe's wife, whom the newspapers described as "a pretty dark-eyed Western co-ed" cried as the verdict was read.

Nearby, Monroe's father, who financed his son's defense in the Bowling Green trial and now was unable to pay a lawyer for his son's federal trial, sat sadly and silently through the procedure, looking down at the floor.

It was over. At 12:45 p.m. on June 2, 1975, Steve Leo Monroe was found guilty.

Two days later on Wednesday, June 4, 1975, at the formal sentencing, Judge Rhodes Bratcher asked Steve Monroe if he had any reason to offer the court why the sentence would not now be pronounced against him in the case?

"No, sir," he replied.

The judge then asked Monroe if he had anything personally to say to the court in his own behalf?

"No, sir," he said again.

After a few questions and comments to defense attorney Fleming, Judge Bratcher asked Monroe if he had a complaint or quarrel with the manner in which any of these matters were handled.

Once again Monroe said, "No, sir."

Just when, for all practical purposes, it looked like the trial was over, Monroe's attorney said he did have one thing to say.

"Your honor, I believe in view of the verdict on count six of the indictment, I'd like to request that any sentence imposed on the other counts run concurrent with the others and concurrent with the sentence on count six," Robert Fleming said.

U.S. District Court Judge Rhodes Bratcher would normally have the authority to pronounce sentencing in federal court cases. However, the federal firearm law allowed for eight men, four women jury to assess life sentences for convictions on charges of exploding illegal devices that result in death. The jury were unanimous.

Then it was Judge Bratcher's turn.

"It is the judgement of the court that this defendant be committed ... "

Monroe was convicted for the bombing of the sales office in Bowling Green and for the death of Peggy Rhodes in her Hardin County house barn on Youngers Creek Road.

The Judge's sentencing mirrored the recommendation of U.S. Attorney Pitt. Counts one through five consecutively for a total of fifty years, to be served concurrently with his life sentence from count six.

Man Given Life In Fatal Bombing

A 24-year-old Bowling Green man was given life in prison after being convicted in U.S. District Court in Louisville Monday on a charge of placing the bomb which killed Mrs. Paul F. (Dusty) Rhodes on her Youngers Creek farm last January.

The federal jury also found Steve Leo Monroe guilty on five other counts of manufacturing, possessing and placing the bomb at the Rhodes farm and another at a mobile home park at Bowling Green in which property was destroyed. Monroe received an additional 10-year prison term on each of these five convictions.

Monroe, who has been held in Jefferson County Jail under heavy bond since his arrest three months ago on charges of violating federal law in connection with the manufacture, possession and placement of the two bombs, has a right to appeal Monday's verdict. He is still in jail in Louisville.

The trial began early last week, and testimony was completed on Friday. Prosecution and defense summations were presented to the jury Monday morning, and the verdict was returned late the same morning. U.S. District Judge Rhodes Bratcher presided at the trial.

Monroe testified last week, but he implicated no one else in the bombings.

One convict serving time in a Michigan prison testified that he helped Monroe manufacture the bomb used in the mobile home park explosion. Another man who is also serving a prison term testified that he saw a bomb in Monroe's transmission shop.

The case concerning the Rhodes bombing is not closed. However, State Detective Walter Sims said, "At this point in time there

are no more leads and no more suspects."

The case was investigated by the Kentucky State Police and the U.S. Treasury Department's Bureau of Alcohol, Tobacco and Firearms.

Monroe was arrested after his fingerprints were found on pieces of the bomb which were found at the scene of the explosion in a barn which killed Mrs. Rhodes and her horse. However, no motive for Monroe to rig the bomb has been established.

Mrs. Peggy Rhodes, 57, was killed, along with her personal riding horse, last Jan. 13 when she opened the stall door in a barn, apparently to feed the horse. Mrs. Rhodes, whose husband operated the Ford agency here for several years, was active in the Elizabethtown Woman's club and in civic affairs.

Pat Osborne, a champion, tunes which will be pl

Headline announcing the life sentence for Steve Monroe.

Judge Rhodes Bratcher

Jim Simon

ATF Special Agent Jerry Benedict

Attorney Bob Fleming

Steve Pitt and his award from the Department of the Treasury.

Carlos Lloyd, 2000.

Bob Bridgewater destroying explosives at Gary Bros. Quarry, 1979.

Bob Bridgewater with Ellis Reed, 1981.

ATF Special Agent Bob Bridgewater at his Bowling Green office.

Tombstone for Paul F. "Dusty" and Peggy Rhodes, 2017.

Bobby Johnson, Jim Johnson's son

Steve Pitt, now the General Councel for the Attorney General's Office in Frankfort, KY.

Carlos Lloyd at the Kentucky State Reformatory in LaGrange, Kentucky.

Attorney Frank E. Haddad, Jr.

Walker Monument in Bowling Green Cemetery

Military marker for Edgar C. Walker

Brochure advertising the Auction of Walkerhurst Farms.

Man testifies Simon, Johnson hired bombing

By RON KAPFHAMMER
News-Enterprise Staff Writer

David Walker, who is serving 10 years for procuring the bombing that killed Mrs. Peggy Rhodes, told a jury in U.S. District Court in Louisville this morning that James R. Simon "is as guilty as I am."

Walker testified that both Simon and James Johnson, partners in the Simon-Johnson Ford Dealership, met with him in a Cave City restaurant around the first of December 1974 and asked him to kill Paul F. "Dusty" Rhodes.

Walker said he agreed to kill Rhodes for a Thunderbird automobile and $10,000. He testified that Johnson had told him that Rhodes had beaten them out of a large sum of money and that he was on the verge of hurting them financially.

Walker said that both Johnson and Simon talked to him on numerous occasions about having Rhodes killed. At one time Simon told him that "time was of the essence."

Other witnesses today depicted the the dealership heavily in debt.

A bookkeeper who worked a year for Simon and Johnson said, "There wasn't any money when I started working and there wasn't any money when it closed."

— James Payton of Citizens Bank said the dealership owed the bank approximately a quarter of a million dollars.

An official of the Ford Motor Credit Corporation said his organization lost $200,000 when the dealership closed. The Ford Motor Credit official said Simon and Johnson had sold cars valued at approximately $100,000 without paying for them. The cars were financed by Ford Motor Credit.

Simon and Johnson also owed Rhodes a note of $128,500 that they assumed when they took over the dealership. They were paying $1,500 a month plus 8½ per cent interest to Rhodes.

Rhodes testified that they owed him $109,000 before they closed.

Rhodes, in testimony yesterday, said he believes Simon tried to kill him in the bomb explosion "for the money" that the automobile dealership would have received from insurance policies on his life that listed the dealership as beneficiary.

Rhodes made the charge when Paul Lewis, one of the defense attorneys, asked Rhodes, in cross examination,

he knew of any reason why Simon, whom Rhodes said had been a friend, would want to harm him.

Rhodes looked at Lewis for a moment, smiled and said that Lewis was putting him on the spot. Then he said he did know of a reason. "For the money," he said.

Rhodes testified that he and Simon had been good friends during the time Simon worked for him when he operated Dusty Rhodes Ford.

Lewis described their relationship in terms of Rhodes taking Simon on as a salesman while Simon "was a kid" and taught him about the automobile business. Simon apparently learned well and soon was sales manager of the dealership and was buying stock in the corporation.

Simon and Jim Johnson, who had worked for Rhodes as a salesman, took over the controlling interest of Dusty Rhodes Ford in September of 1972, Rhodes said.

Simon already owned enough stock that he did not have to put up any money in the transaction, Rhodes said.

Johnson had to buy a new stock issue, though, and the corporation had to buy up shares of stock that Rhodes controlled as president of the corporation.

The amount of the transaction was $180,000 that the corporation owed Rhodes.

Rhodes bought back the farm implement dealership from the corporation, reducing the amount owed to him to $128,500.

Rhodes, Simon and Johnson entered into a security agreement that said the corporation would maintain a life insurance policy on his life for the amount of the note with his wife named beneficiary.

Rhodes said he wanted this done so that his wife would receive the money if something happened to him.

Rhodes said he had three life insurance policies assigned to Citizens Bank in Elizabethtown to secure a small business loan. He said the business loan was a corporation indebtedness that Simon and Johnson were assuming.

He said his three life insurance policies were supposed to be replaced by policies on the lives of Simon and Johnson and that the beneficiary on Rhodes' policies was supposed to be changed to his wife.

This never happened, Rhodes said.

Simon, Johnson accused in Rhodes bombing death

By RON KAPFHAMMER
News-Enterprise Staff Writer

Agents of the Bureau of Alcohol, Tobacco and Firearms and the Kentucky State Police arrested James R. Simon last night in the 200 block of Terry Court and charged the former Elizabethtown automobile dealer with being a co-conspirator in the Jan. 13, 1976 bombing death of Mrs. Paul F. Rhodes.

The ATF agents were acting upon an indictment issued earlier in the day by a federal grand jury that charged that both Simon and the late James Johnson, his partner in the Simon-Johnson Ford agency, conspired with three Bowling Green men to place the bomb on the Rhodes farm near Elizabethtown.

Johnson died last May of carbon monoxide poisoning, an apparent suicide, while one of the Bowling

Green men connected with the bombing, Steve Leo Monroe, was being tried in U.S. District Court in Louisville. Monroe is serving a life sentence for his part in the bombing.

Simon was taken to Louisville last night where he was jailed as a federal prisoner. Bond was set at $30,000 but Simon had not posted bail early this morning, according to the U.S. Court clerk's office in Louisville.

Simon was charged with both conspiring in the bombing and with aiding and abetting in the bombing that caused the death of Mrs. Rhodes.

The conspiracy charge carries a maximum sentence of five years but the second charge carries a maximum sentence of life in a federal penitentiary.

Simon will be arraigned on Friday, Feb. 13, which is exactly one year and one month since the death of Mrs.

Rhodes. U.S. Magistrate Rhodes Bratcher, who presided over the Monroe trial, will set a trial date at the arraignment.

The trial will be in Federal Court in Louisville.

ATF agents Bill Rockliff, who has been working actively on the Rhodes bombing case for about a year, and Frank Guernsey and Kentucky State Police Lt. Walter Sims told the arrest of Simon apparently closes out the Rhodes bombing investigation.

"I hope it does, anyway. It's been piecemeal every step of the way. It's been a long, rough case," Guernsey said.

Sims said the agents moved in on Simon at about 8:30 p.m. yesterday while he was still in his parked car at the 200 block of Terry Court.

Sims said Simon apparently had not expected them and seemed surprised

when they closed in. Simon did not issue any statements, Sims said.

Simon has been a real estate salesman working out of the John Simon Agency since late last year.

The Simon-Johnson Ford dealership was forced to close earlier in the year. The apparent motive for the bombing was an insurance policy on Paul F. "Dusty" Rhodes that would have paid over $100,000 to the dealership had Rhodes died.

Rhodes, who sold the dealership to Simon and Johnson and was still involved in the business at the time of the bombing, apparently was the intended victim of the bomb.

Two other Bowling Green men who pleaded guilty last month for their roles in the bombing soon will be sentenced formally by U.S. Judge

(Continued on Page 2)

The News-Enterprise

CECILIA GLENDALE   *Elizabethtown, Radcliff, Fort Knox, Vine Grove*   SONORA UPTON

TUESDAY, FEB. 18, 1976   Elizabethtown 769-2312 — Phone — Radcliff 351-1131   VOLUME 3, NO. 111 - 15 CENTS

Men plead guilty in Rhodes bombing

By RON KAPFHAMMER
News-Enterprise Staff Writer

Two Bowling Green men pleaded guilty this morning in U.S. District Court to charges connected with the bombing death of Mrs. Peggy Rhodes.

Carlos Calvin Lloyd, 29, changed his plea at around 9:30 and agreed to testify against David Cooper Walker, 47, according to Lloyd's attorney. Lloyd told federal prosecutors that he possibly could implicate two others in the case.

Walker changed his plea to guilty later this morning.

Lloyd is charged with helping Steve Leo Monroe, who is serving a life sentence for his alleged role in the bombing, manufacture, place, and detonate the bomb that killed Mrs. Rhodes.

Walker is charged with ... ng and abetting in the explosion and with having "induced" the bombing.

Both men could have received life sentences if convicted by a jury.

Lloyd agreed to change his plea and accept a sentence of 18 years to run concurrently with sentences he will

soon start serving from previous convictions. He agreed to dismiss his appeals in cases in the Alabama Federal District Court and in Warren County, Ky.

The federal court has agreed not to prosecute Lloyd for any stolen-car related charges.

Walker agreed to accept a 10-year sentence.

Formal sentencing will take place later in the month.

Lloyd and Walker will testify next week before a federal grand jury concerning the Rhodes bombing case.

Federal prosecutors have not revealed whom Lloyd and Walker claim they can implicate in the bombing.

Mrs. Rhodes, 57, the wife of former Elizabethtown new car dealer, Paul F. (Dusty) Rhodes, was killed Jan. 13, 1975. She was killed by a bomb that allegedly was rigged by Monroe and Lloyd to explode when she opened a stall door in a barn at the Rhodes farm off Younger's Creek Road in Hardin County.

Men plead guilty in Rhodes bombing

153

Jim Johnson smoking his pipe.

Reporter Ron Kapfhammer, himself, became a part of the investigation and trial due to his accurate reporting. He left the E'town paper not long after the last trial, and at one time served as press secretary for John Y. Brown before he was elected governor of Kentucky. He died at the age of 50 in 1999.

News-Enterprise reporter Ron Kapfhammer shakes hands with Kentucky Congressman William Natcher.

Jerry Benedict (left) and William Rockliff, ATF agents from Louisville, receive an award in 1976.

Jim Simon (front center) with his 1955-56 Elizabethtown Catholic High School Basketball Team

From
Steve Monroe

75-1376-L
(JW)

Dear Mr. Pitt

I'm terribly worried about my future sir. I'm a nervous wreck from worries of what may happen to me once I go to the penitentiary. It may seem as a simple thing to many people really a very complex situation. I have cooperated with the F.B.I. in naming over thirty five names of people who are business men in organized crime. Half of these men are in federal penitentiaries now and all of them know I am talking. I have watched what they have planned for other people who were talking. One such person is already dead. His name is Donald Barnes from Bowling Green. They say his wife shot him, but I know different. Honest to God Mr. Pitt, if I step foot in penitentiary after this, I'm just a walking corpse. For God's sake, please believe me. I'm really not very worried about Walker or Loid. I'm worried about these other people. I know for a fact they are going to silence me strickly for protection, even if it never does go to trial. They are type that makes sure, it doesn't go to trial. They don't know how much I know and they won't take any chances on it. The A.T.F. doesn't realize what I have gotten myself into because they don't and won't colaborate with the F.B.I.. It's like two large worlds that won't focus to make it one for me. The marshals don't realize how much danger I am in or they would have never wanted to send me to Terra Haute. My God Mr. Pitt, with all of this confusion between people, how on God's earth remain calm without fearing for my very life? When I was in Terre Haute, it took only two days for information to travel from Terminal Island to Terre Haute. From Calif. to Ky. by grapvine in fourty eight hours.

Page two

The main reason I couldn't accept immunity is I was afraid of what would happen to me. I knew for a fact that I would be convicted. I have been tricked by the law so many times I was afraid you wouldn't hold to your part and I would be thrown in a penitentiary anyway.

These people don't think twice if they concider to murder someone, I know because I have worked with them for many years.

If there is anyway in the world that I can receive a parole from the judge without having to go to a penitentiary, I can promise you from the very deepest part of my heart sir, I will never, ever, ever, become involved with anything against the law. I mean that more than anything I have ever said in my life Mr. Pitt. If I could only be given a chance to prove this, I would go back to college and get a degree in business, or journalism and inrole in law school afterwards. If for one moment, I stray from this goal, I'll return to the penitentiary, no questions asked.

Sir, I know I'm as good as dead if I ever set foot in a federal penitentiary in the United States. The going price for a set murder in the penitentiary is three cartons of cigarettes. I know this is true sir, because I worked in the hospital in Terre Haute. I have never, ever had any type of disaplinary action ever even concidered against me in my incarceration, that started over fifteen months ago.

Sincerly Yours
Steve

Letter from Steve Monroe to Steve Pitt.

Ford dealership up for grabs

Ford Motor Company is expected to name a new dealer for Elizabethtown this week to take over Simon-Johnson Ford.

Until Ford announces a new dealer, the Ford franchise remains in the name of Elizabethtown businessmen Jim Simon and James Johnson, a spokesman for Ford told The News-Enterprise.

"It is still a Simon-Johnson franchise as far as the Ford Motor Company is concerned," Richard Anderson, assistant sales manager of Ford's Louisville office, said.

Anderson said whatever financial arrangements exist between Simon-Johnson and Dusty Rhodes is "their business." Rhodes kept the doors of the dealership open last week and ran advertisements for a "Repossession Sale."

A Ford Motor spokesman said he was not aware that telephone calls were being answered "Dusty Rhodes Ford" at the dealership.

"They have no authority (to transfer a franchise)," a spokesman from Ford's Atlanta office said. "They (Simon and Johnson) would either resign or we would terminate them. They are still the dealers of record."

Dusty Rhodes, who owned the dealership before selling it to Simon and Johnson, has formed a corporation named "Dusty Rhodes Ford" and the receptionist at the office last week answered the telephone "Dusty Rhodes Ford."

Despite appearances, Rhodes does not own the Ford dealership.

Rhodes said he has applied for the dealership along with "four or five others" and incorporated simply "to get the thing started."

Rhodes said he has leased the building and is selling the cars remaining on the Simon-Johnson lot to which financed the wholesale purchase of most of the cars.

Rhodes said Simon and Johnson have resigned the Ford dealership.

"The doors would be closed if it weren't for me. Nobody would be here selling these cars if I didn't keep the doors open," Rhodes said.

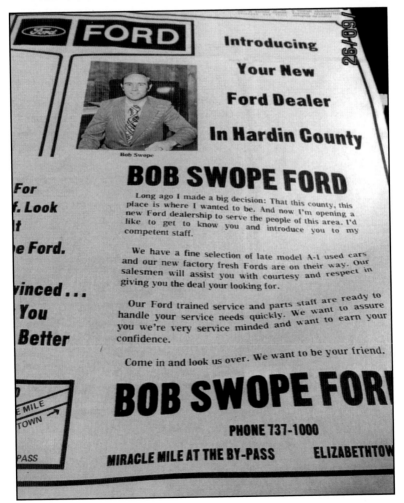

Bob Swope Ford

espondent, ill, Jim Johnson ends his life; uneral services held here on 46th birthday

Left: Johnson ends life.

The News - Enterprise

E'town 769-2312; Radcliff 351-1181   Hardin County's most widely read newspaper   June 25-25, 1978; Vol. 2, No. 205—15 cents

Jury finds local man not guilty

Simon cleared of charges

Newspaper headline

Author Gary West and the stack of transcripts he used to research and verify the truth behind the Youngers Creek Road bombing.

Youngers Creek sign on Bluegrass Parkway

Ruth, daughter of Peggy and Dusty Rhodes at the family monument.

CHAPTER NINETEEN

One day after Steve Monroe's trail began in Louisville, the Peggy Rhodes case took a sudden turn that added a missing piece to the puzzle.

In Elizabethtown, the residents were following the murder case so intently that it was the topic of conversation at any gathering of two or more people.

Surely someone had hired these three guys from Bowling Green to kill Peggy Rhodes. But the strong scuttlebutt in town was that maybe it wasn't Peggy who they really wanted to kill.

On May 29, 1975, just as the Monroe trial got underway, Jim Johnson, the former Kentucky State Trooper and former Sheriff of Logan County who had become the county's pride and joy, was found dead in his car in a closed garage at his Elizabethtown home.

Unofficially, he tried to take his own life twice before.

In late March 1975, Johnson went back to Russellville for a visit, where he talked to friends and did an interview with the *Logan-Leader* newspaper about his failed negotiations to buy back the Ford dealership there. He told the paper that he had not given up hope of buying the franchise at a later time. According to the newspaper, Johnson said he planned on returning to Russellville to operate a used-car business.

As Johnson drove back to Elizabethtown that Sunday night, March 23, he crashed into a concrete abutment just south of the toll booth plaza on the Kentucky Turnpike. He was taken to Hardin Memorial Hospital. The wreck, according to Johnson, was a result of a truck forcing him off the road during a rainstorm. With a broken kneecap, bruised lungs, broken ribs, broken collarbone, and a broken leg, he spent several days in the hospital.

There were those in Elizabethtown who thought Johnson's accident was no accident at all but an attempt to take his own life.

ATF Agent Bridgewater was a friend of Johnson's from their law enforcement days. "He called my house. He was crying, crazy-like," recalled Bridgewater. "I told him I'd get by to see him. When I got there he had a hospital bed in his home, recovering from his wreck."

Bridgewater recalled that Eugene Coffey, a state police friend, stopped by and gave Johnson a Bible that had belonged to his mother.

"I stood back and listened ... didn't say anything. I really feel like Jimmy (Johnson) was ready to make a confession until Coffey showed up. I didn't particularly like doing the investigation on him because we were friends, but it was my job," said Bridgewater.

It was several weeks later in late April that Johnson was found unconscious in his garage, apparently overcome by carbon monoxide. Although he was revived, it was once more thought to have been a failed attempt to take his own life.

On May 29, the former lawman who had had a hand in starting Trooper Island, among several positive projects in his more than twenty-year career, finally was successful in a suicide.

Martha, his wife, found her husband in his car in the garage with the motor running. He was holding an open Bible with a note he had written on the back of two envelopes.

Bobby Johnson, Jim and Martha's son, was eighteeen at the time and remembers the note:

I talked to God and God knows my problems. People are talking and I didn't have anything to do with Peggy. You're going to hear bad things about me, but it's not true. Bobby help your brothers and mother. I'm sorry for everything. I hope you will find a nice man to marry. Tell Bob and Shirl (Jim's brother and his wife) I'm sorry. They'll (the dealership) take the cars tomorrow. I love you, I love you, I love you.

The news of Jim Johnson's death spread quickly in not only Elizabethtown but also in Russellville. Bobby Johnson tried to piece it all together. He knew he needed to be strong for his mother and two younger brothers.

"After Jimmy killed himself, I went to the visitation in Logan County," Agent Bridgewater said. "I could actually hear the whispers and comments about 'What's he doing here?' Jimmy Johnson was my friend, but I didn't go to the funeral."

Jim Johnson was buried on what would have been his forty-sixth birthday.

Bobby Johnson had seen the financial demise of Simon-Johnson Ford from the edge. He had worked there part-time, doing whatever he was told to do. And there were times he rode along with his dad to discuss a little business with friends. Mentally he was putting together things he had heard and seen. It was a struggle for the young man who worshipped his dad but by his own admission later said he really didn't know his father.

As stories began to unfold after the murder of Peggy Rhodes, Bobby found it difficult to believe his dad was involved in any way. The rumors were all over and finally Bobby Johnson went to ATF Agent Bridgewater to see if it was possible.

"Bob Bridgewater showed me a book of photos, and one of them was a guy I had seen my dad with. It was David Walker," Bobby Johnson recalled. "We went to lunch at the Ramada Inn on Hurstbourne Lane in Louisville. Looking back on it, I can't believe my dad took me with them."

Bobby Johnson continued:

"They talked about Walker getting his mother Irene's money to re-purchase the Ford dealership in Russellville. It was so creepy. Walker sat in the back, and he asked dad if he ever smoked pot. 'Nothing like smoking pot after sex,' he said. "I told dad later I didn't like that guy. Dad told me not to tell anybody about going to Louisville with Walker.

"I heard lots of stories and saw a few things since I worked part-time at the dealership. I heard Jim Simon say, 'If we can't get the money I will take it out of his (Dusty's) hide.'"

Over the years Bobby Johnson, in looking back on those horrible years with the death of family friend Peggy Rhodes and the suicide of his father, at times has had difficulty sorting through it all. He was never quite sure how much his uncle Bob, a Bowling Green banker, actually knew.

"Uncle Bob was paranoid about me keeping quiet and not talking about anything I heard," he said. "And then he told me my dad and John Bryant (Dixie Liquors) were tight and that my dad was getting a kickback for letting some of John's liquor get into Logan County when he was sheriff."

When all the investigations started in the murder of Peggy Rhodes, Bobby Johnson developed a friendship with ATF agents William Rockliff and Bridgewater.

Agent Rockliff remembered conversations with the younger Johnson. "I think he was majoring in criminal justice and even worked for the state police part-time while in college," Rockliff said. "He was interested in becoming an ATF agent."

"We talked several times about his future as an FBI or ATF agent," offered Bridgewater.

Bobby Johnson had graduated from Russellville High School in 1973 and wanted to attend college at Western Kentucky University in Bowling Green.

"My dad said no. He said the town was too bad, so I went to UK Community College in E-town and later to Western," he said.

Now, of all those conversations he had had with his dad, while some were still confusing, some began to make sense.

"Dad told mom one time he could have her bumped off for a $1,000. Mom would giggle, but later on, she said he probably could because he knew half of the underworld in Kentucky."

Even though Jim Johnson and Jim Simon passed a lie detector test early in the investigation, Bobby Johnson couldn't help but remember his dad telling him how the test could be fooled.

"He said if a person put a rock in the bottom of his shoe ... press on the rock and concentrate on it, it would work. Dad said he'd seen it done," Bobby Johnson said.

"My dad had a bad temper. He was difficult for me to work for. He talked to everyone at work like an angel, but me, he talked to like a dog."

As bad as things were financially for Jim Johnson, he refused to file for bankruptcy. He had an image to uphold and he wanted to save his Ford dealership at all cost.

Friends in Russellville had said Jim would be in position to get a good state job in Frankfort. He had a good reputation, and that was most important to him. It was talked about that Gov. Bert Combs even considered naming Jim Johnson as the State Police Commissioner at one time.

Al Smith, editor of the *Logan Leader* newspaper in Russellville, who later went on to fame with KET (Kentucky Education Television), was a good friend of Johnson's back when he owned the Ford dealership and later became sheriff of Logan County.

Saying that Smith felt betrayed by his friend would be an understatement. A more descriptive word would be *duped*. In the beginning of it all, Smith wrote praising stories about the former sheriff.

"G.C. McMillen was a state police detective friend of mine, and he told me to tread carefully on any stories I wrote about Jimmy Johnson," Smith remembered. "I was warned not to get too involved. I just failed to grab hold of what might be the implications about the truth early on."

After Johnson's wreck back in late March driving home from Russellville, Smith was one of the first to call his friend at the hospital in Elizabethtown.

"At the time I really didn't know he was connected (to the murder)," said Smith. "Some in town (Russellville) thought Jimmy was like mercury in a skillet."

For Bobby Johnson, his mother, and his younger brothers, the memories of what seemed to be a good, if not perfect, life don't ever go away. And then to have it shattered by a father you loved, respected, and looked up to just didn't make sense to a teenager ready to begin his own life in a profession he was drawn to by his dad.

"It was so depressing," Bobby Johnson recalled years later. "So many thoughts raced through my mind. Peggy Rhodes. Why? Then I found out my dad and Jim Simon thought Walker was going to shoot Dusty from a tree line … not a bomb. I would have rather seen my dad dead than in prison. It may not be right and sounds kind of cold, but it's true."

CHAPTER TWENTY

S till with no motive, it looked like Steve Leo Monroe was willing to keep his mouth shut, as he was sent off to the Jefferson County Jail in Louisville, where he would await assignment to a federal penitentiary.

There was no law that said a jury could not convict a murderer without a motive. They only had to know he did it. Steve Monroe fit the bill.

With Monroe's trial over, his court-appointed attorney, Robert Fleming submitted his fee voucher for defending his client to the court. Fleming documented his hours and asked for $1,397.50. That amount was declined, and he was paid $1,000.00.

Monroe, after spending three months in jail awaiting trial, now faced another fifty years in prison. The cocky arrogance he exhibited during his trial was beginning to fade as reality set in.

The federal penitentiary in Terre Haute, Indiana, was where Monroe was sent. His emotions were up and down like an elevator, and at one time, he was placed in isolation because of his fear of reprisal for what some of his partners in crime thought he might have already revealed about their criminal activities.

Six weeks into his stay at Terre Haute, Monroe was re-thinking everything. Having gotten word to the outside that he was willing to keep his mouth shut, he asked for some "silence money." But he didn't get it.

"I went to visit him in Terre Haute four or five times," said Agent Bridgewater. "He would be all emotional, crying and all, and then the next time he would have an attitude … like he was one coldhearted guy. I told him I'd try to help him if he came clean with everything. He wasn't talking. I stood up and told him I didn't care if he rotted here, and I got up and left.

"That night when I got home back in Bowling Green on a Friday night about 11 o'clock, I got a phone call from the main prison guard at the prison. He said Monroe was going crazy and wanted to talk."

When the following Monday rolled around, Bridgewater was on his way back to Terre Haute.

"When I got there he started shaking like he was possessed," Bridgewater said. "He gave me a full confession, even saying he was involved in the car theft ring in Bowling Green. He told me about the two Corvettes he and (Carlos) Lloyd had stolen, as well as all of the other cars and trucks."

With Monroe's turnaround, it now looked like a possible motive would be discovered as to why anyone would want to kill Peggy Rhodes.

Although Bowling Green for years had become known as a place where people blew things up, in actuality, explosives had become a part of the anti-war movement in the 1970s across America. Introduced mainly in big cities and primarily blowing up government buildings, a terrorist group called the Weatherman took responsibility for it.

On June 10, 1976, from Terre Haute Penitentiary, Monroe sent a bizarre two-page handwritten letter on legal paper to Assistant U.S. Attorney Steve Pitt, who had prosecuted him for the Peggy Rhodes murder and bombing of the mobile home sales office in Bowling Green. Unlike the letter Monroe sent to Agent Bridgewater from the Jefferson County Jail where his greeting was "Bob," this one opened with "Dear Mr. Pitt." The letter was written in perfect penmanship, and though there were several misspelled words and an occasional misuse of English, it was generally well written, especially when you consider that Monroe had to repeat his freshman year at Warren Central High School in 1964.

Monroe, in the letter, begged Pitt for help, saying, "If I step foot in a federal penitentiary after this (Terre Haute), I'm just a walking corpse."

He went on: "I have cooperated with the FBI in naming over thirty-five names of people who are business men in organized crime. These people don't think twice if they decide to murder someone, I know because I have worked with them for many years."

And then on page two, apparently forgetting that he had blown an innocent lady to smithereens, he wrote, "If there is anyway in the world I can receive a parole from the judge without having to go to the penitentiary, I can promise you from the very deepest part of my heart sir, I will never, ever, ever become involved with anything against the law."

He continued: "I would go back to college and get a degree in business or journalism and enroll in law school afterwards."

Now U.S. Marshalls brought Monroe back to Louisville to officially be interviewed and to find out who or who all was behind the murder on Youngers Creek Road.

Six weeks after Monroe was convicted and when he finally realized the "silence money" he requested would not be coming, he sent word he had a little more of the story to tell. And he told it all. He told of being contacted by David Walker to assist in the elimination of an Elizabethtown car dealer, Dusty Rhodes. He went on to say he had brought in Carlos Lloyd to help carry it out.

Steve Monroe began to weave his story in hopes of getting some time knocked off his fifty-year prison sentence.

For several months Carlos Lloyd and David Walker had been on edge. Walker even tried to get more money to Monroe's family in hopes that they would keep him quiet.

"Larry Gann told me when they arrested Steve, so I knew it wouldn't be long before they came looking for me," Lloyd said years later during a prison interview in LaGrange. "I had a premonition, so I sold my car. Subconsciously, I felt like my arrest was coming."

He was right. On Saturday night, September 22, 1975, Agent Bob Bridgewater and several other agents moved in on Carlos Lloyd. It was 9 p.m.

"I was at the College Street Inn (Bowling Green) with my girlfriend," Lloyd said. "They throwed my hands behind my back and picked me plumb up off the floor. My girlfriend was screaming, 'Let him go, let him go!' They were roughing me up when they put me in the police car, and Bridgewater told them to cool it. 'He's not causing any trouble.'"

Lloyd was taken to the old county jail next to the courthouse in Bowling Green.

A few hours later, Bridgewater and his associates moved in on David Walker. It was shortly after midnight when they knocked on his Memphis Junction home in Bowling Green and took him into custody.

The ATF and Kentucky State Police had worked feverishly to solve the Peggy Rhodes murder and the chief supplier of information was Steve Monroe.

Lloyd and Walker spent a few days in the Bowling Green jail before being transferred to the Jefferson County Jail in Louisville.

"They offered me immunity from prosecution," Lloyd recalled. "I told them I didn't think Steve did it. I was a big tough guy then ... and I wasn't talking."

Walker's age was listed at forty-seven, and his occupation was secretary of the Walker Associates Land Development Corporation of Bowling Green and sometime truck driver. Lloyd, twenty-eight, said he himself worked as a carpenter, plumber, truck driver, and general laborer.

At their arraignment before U.S. District Court Judge Dale R. Booth, the two were appointed attorneys, and their bail was set at $150,000 each. It was then that Agent Bridgewater said he received a call from Irene Walker, David's mother, who in past years had used her wealth to get her son out of trouble. But, now, murder was a different story.

"She asked how serious it was." Bridgewater said. "I told her David was involved, or I wouldn't have arrested him. She expressed remorse about Peggy Rhodes getting killed. She wanted to know if he was guilty before she posted bond."

She didn't, and her son David Cooper Walker was on his own.

State Police Lt. Detective Walter Sims announced in a press conference that Walker and Lloyd would have their cases heard by the federal grand jury on October 16, less than a month after they were arrested.

Sims went on to say that if the grand jury did indict Walker and Lloyd, their trial dates "may be set for late October or early November."

Walker and Lloyd pleaded not guilty.

However, as the two were learning more and more about the case, evidence began to pile up, and the pressure of being the one to tough it out and be left holding the bag began to creep into their way of dealing with what they now faced. Authorities for the prosecution felt like it was only a matter of time before Carlos Lloyd and David Walker would come clean.

Carlos Lloyd, at 9:30 a.m. on January 6, 1976, a few days shy of one year since Peggy Rhodes died, was the first to change his plea to guilty and agreed to testify against David Walker. Lloyd then told federal agents he could possibly implicate two others in the murder.

It was only a couple of hours later that Walker changed his plea to guilty.

Lloyd was charged with helping Steve Monroe manufacture, place, and detonate the bomb that killed Peggy Rhodes. Walker was charged with aiding and abetting in the explosion and with having induced the bombing. Both men were set to go on trial before U.S. District Court Judge Charles Allen and could have received life sentences if convicted by a jury.

In changing his plea, Lloyd agreed to accept a sentence of eighteen years to run concurrently with sentences he faced from crimes he committed in Alabama and Bowling Green.

David Walker agreed to accept a ten-year sentence.

He pleaded guilty to conspiring to damage a building involved in interstate commerce by an explosive that caused the death and unlawfully conspiring in making a bomb whose manufacturing he helped to induce. The two counts each carried ten years to be served concurrently.

Because of Steve Monroe's cooperation, federal agents were able to move on Walker and Lloyd. They had pled guilty, and Monroe's "please help me" letter to Assistant U.S. Attorney Steve Pitt had worked. Well, not really.

Monroe didn't get paroled as he requested, but he did get, with Pitt's blessing, a favorable ruling from Judge Rhodes Bratcher that reduced his sentence from fifty to twenty years. He was re-sentenced on July 29, 1976.

The dragnet was still tightening.

Police and ATF agents had been investigating now for some eleven months, much of it out of the public's eye.

Informed sources told *Elizabethtown News-Enterprise* reporter Ron Kapfhammer that police believe the order for the bombing originated in Elizabethtown and that Walker allegedly was the "middle payoff man" who arranged for the bombing to be done.

Kapfhammer went on to write that his source said the police think they "have a fairly good idea of what happened," but that some crucial points in the line of events that led to Mrs. Rhodes' violent death "are still a little cloudy."

The sources went on to say police were optimistic that they will be able to answer most of the key questions of the investigation.

Walker and Lloyd both spent several days in the Louisville jail before being transferred. Walker went to the federal prison in Leavenworth, Kansas, while Lloyd went to Terre Haute before being moved to Atlanta Federal Penitentiary, where he stayed for five years. The feds then moved him to Talladega, Alabama.

Walker's young wife did her best to stay in contact with him, even making the long drive from Bowling Green to Kansas when she could. It was on one of those visits to Leavenworth during his six-year stay there that she recalled her husband asking her to do something she wasn't comfortable with.

"David was always in control," she said. "One of my visits was a two-day visit, and Irene (David's mother) was with me. We were permitted to touch, hold hands, and even kiss. The first day he demanded that I slip two $20 bills to him the next day.

"He told me when I got back to the motel, get an iron from the maid … get some cellophane and tightly roll separately two bills in the cellophane, take the hot iron, and seal them. When I came to visit him the next day when I kissed him, I was to transfer them from my mouth to his. When I didn't do it, he got very angry."

She went on to say she knew they were being watched, and since money was considered a contraband, she didn't want to become part of his scheme, no matter how much she loved him.

Later when she and Irene left the prison, she told her mother-in-law what her son wanted her to do and that she had refused.

"She said, 'Good, you're not as big of a fool as I thought you were.'"

Walker did the six years at Leavenworth before going to Memphis, where he served out his time.

Still no motive as to why David Walker, Steve Monroe, and Carlos Lloyd, all from Bowling Green, had conspired to make a bomb and kill Peggy Rhodes in Elizabethtown.

But that was about to change. Local rumors were all over Hardin County.

Everyone seemed to have an opinion as to why Peggy Rhodes died on her farm on Youngers Creek Road.

CHAPTER TWENTY-ONE

J im Johnson's death was a shock to his friends in Russellville but not so much to those in Elizabethtown who knew him.

The murder of Peggy Rhodes had been peeled away in layers, much like that of an onion. The talk had moved beyond whispers and rumors about who was really behind David Walker and the two men whom he had hired, Steve Monroe and Carlos Lloyd, to carry out the contract killing, not on Peggy Rhodes but the real intended target, her husband Dusty.

One of Johnson's friends, who had known him for years, said what many of those following the case thought.

"The only way out for the man who had created his own nightmare was suicide," he said. "That left only one conclusion for such an act—that was an admission of guilt."

Even though Jim Johnson and Jim Simon had passed a state police lie-detector test about Peggy Rhodes' death "with flying colors," according to Lt. Walter Sims. Federal agents, however, weren't so sure and continued to consider the two prime suspects. The federal agents did not use lie-detector test in their investigations because of their unreliability as evidence in trials.

David Walker's testimony would be key to providing the unanswered questions of "why Peggy Rhodes?" for the last several months.

With Monroe in prison from a trial conviction, Walker and Lloyd agreeing to a plea deal and prison terms, and Jim Johnson dead, it left only Jim Simon.

On Monday, February 9, 1976, at 5:30 p.m., ATF agents and Kentucky State Police troopers surprised the forty-two-year-old Simon while he was sitting in his parked car in the 200 block of Terry Court in Elizabethtown.

ATF was acting on an indictment issued earlier that same day by a federal grand jury in Louisville. The indictment charged both

Simon and Jim Johnson who had taken his own life several months before.

Simon was immediately taken to Louisville, where he was jailed as a federal prisoner. Bond was set at $20,000.

The charge against him was conspiring to the bombing and with aiding and abetting in the bombing that killed Peggy Rhodes. The lesser charge, conspiracy, carried a maximum sentence of five years; however, the second charge carried a maximum sentence of life in federal penitentiary.

Jim Simon's arraignment came on Friday, February 13, one year and one month to the day since the Rhodes death.

The *Elizabethtown News-Enterprise* carried a large banner headline above the masthead reading: "Simon, Johnson Accused in Rhodes Bombing Death."

For some in the community, it was shocking, but for many, they thought they had already figured it out.

ATF Agents Bill Rockliff, who had been working on the case from almost the very beginning, and Frank Guernsey, and Kentucky State Police Lt. Walter Sims reported, "the arrest of Simon apparently closes out the Rhodes bombing investigation."

"I hope it does, anyway. It's been piecemeal every step of the way," Agent Guernsey told *News-Enterprise* reporter Ron Kapfhammer. "It's been a long rough case."

In the meantime the Ford dealership, owned first by Dusty Rhodes and then Jim Simon and Jim Johnson, had been in turmoil.

Dusty Rhodes, in an effort to keep the doors open because he was still owed money, ran some local advertising for a "Repossession Sale." And phone calls to the dealership were being answered, "Dusty Rhodes Ford."

"It is still a Simon-Johnson franchise as far as Ford Motor Company is concerned," Richard Anderson, assistant sales manager of Ford's Louisville office, said at the time.

Rhodes had formed a new corporation to try to re-establish himself as the owner, but despite appearances, Rhodes did not own the Ford dealership according to Ford Motor Company.

Rhodes said he was selling cars remaining on the Simon-Johnson lot to repay Ford Motor Credit, which had financed the wholesale purchase of most of the cars.

"The doors would be closed if it weren't for me," Rhodes added. "Nobody would be here selling these cars if I didn't keep the doors open."

With the Elizabethtown Ford dealership apparently up for grabs, there were several interested parties, with Dusty being one of them. However, in 1975, Bob Swope, at the age of twenty-seven, became the youngest Ford dealer in the nation.

The dealership had been a mess before and after the death of Peggy Rhodes, so now Ford was making sure the next dealer could put things on sound footing.

"Dad asked me if I was ready to be a Ford dealer," Bob Swope recalled. "You have few chances like this, and I had so much help from my dad Bill and uncle Sam Swope.

"Dusty was very helpful to dad and me in paving the way with Ford Motor Company," Bob Swope said.

Rhodes' iconic white cowboy hat and cigar-chomping had for years become his signature, and by most accounts to the car-buying public, he was a character.

"Part of the transfer deal with us was to furnish Dusty with a full-loaded Ford LTD Landeau annually for five years," continued Swope. "He really helped us, and we were glad to do it."

By now the Ford dealership was the least of Jim Simon's worries. Soon after getting out of the car business, he became a realtor in town. In fact, when he was arrested, that was listed as his occupation.

But now ATF and Kentucky State Police knew they finally had proof of guilt, as well as the motive. The insurance policy on Dusty Rhodes' life would pay $150,000 to the Simon-Johnson Ford dealership in the event of Dusty's death. So, now it had become clear that Dusty, not wife Peggy, was the intended victim of the bomb.

Dusty Rhodes, however, was not the first Elizabethtown car dealer to have had an attempt made on his life.

On October 24, 1938, George W. Woodard was shot as he sat in his car on Mulberry Street in broad daylight at 9 a.m. near the downtown Masonic Temple. The shooter, thirty-five-year-old F. W. Gabbert, fired two shots into Woodward's car, one of which hit him. It was said Gabbert had been a former employee at Woodward Motors and the two had argued over money.

After being shot, the forty-eight-year-old Woodward drove himself to Dr. R. D. Layman's office to be examined. Thirty minutes later, Woodard, with his wife and the doctor were headed to St. Anthony Hospital in Louisville, where George Woodard died from the gunshot.

He had been an automobile dealer for eighteen years, with dealerships in Leitchfield and Horse Cave, Kentucky.

CHAPTER TWENTY-TWO

O
n February 13, 1976, James R. Simon pleaded not guilty in U. S. District Court in Louisville to any and everything to do with the death of Peggy Rhodes.

U. S. District Judge Rhodes Bratcher set the trial date for April 12, 1976. But like so many times in dealing with courts of law, delays can and do become the norm. Finally on June 19, 1976, Simon's trial got underway.

When Jim and his family hired Louisville attorney Frank Haddad, many felt they had hired the best money could buy. Not just the best in Kentucky but the best attorney, period. His fees were reported at $150 to $300 an hour and, for some cases, fixed fees as high as $200,000.

Haddad was born in Louisville in the old Haymarket District on Jefferson Street in 1928 to Lebanese immigrants. His very name came to stand for a client in serious trouble. Books and lots of newspaper stories have been written about him.

(In 1990, he represented another Elizabethtown citizen, Dr. Fred Rainey, who received shock probation for several sex crimes, and then in 1986, Haddad won an acquittal for Bowling Green's Dr. Tom Hall for conspiracy to murder his wife.)

The money to secure the services of a lawyer like Frank Haddad was said to have come from Jim's mother and stepfather, James Corbett, who had put up Simon's $20,000 appearance bond.

Haddad believed a lawyer's whole-hearted commitment to his client's cause was a professional and moral obligation. And he, himself, was guilty of saying a person is never guilty until the jury says he is guilty.

Courier-Journal columnist Bob Hill wrote this about Haddad: "No one worked harder on a case than Frank Haddad," at least that's what dozens of lawyers and a few judges who knew him said.

"Haddad's voice was said to be hypnotic, soothing, perfectly modulated that kept anyone in earshot in place. His steady gaze and slow pace were all a part of the schtick. His pause for effect could have a court room in the palm of his hand."

"With somewhat of an owlish-look and his well-known wisdom, Frank Haddad was the attorney you hired if you were guilty … and could afford him. That was the perception, but perception is not always the truth."

Haddad was even known to ask the jury the question, "'If you're guilty, get Frank Haddad.' Do any of you believe that way?

"In a career that began in 1952, when he walked into the court room he knew every fact in the case. His reputation was so good, often judges didn't want to be accused of favoritism."

With the Peggy Rhodes' case so strong that three were already in prison with enough evidence to convict and another of the accused had taken his own life, Haddad had his work cut out for him.

Early in the investigation ATF Agent William Rockliff said Simon did not take his possibility of being charged in the Rhodes death seriously until he was arrested. In fact on that night, Simon asked federal and state agents making the arrest if they were serious. Rockliff went on to tell him they were very serious, and Simon again said he could not believe it.

Trial lawyers know much of their work begins well before they lay out their case before a sitting jury. Some even say, "Getting the right jury" is paramount to them winning or losing.

When jury pools are summoned "for duty," they are told, "trial by jury of one's peers is a sacred right of every American and the cornerstone of our judicial system." The process of selecting a jury is referred to as *voir dire*, which means a judge or counsel can question potential jurors regarding biases, objectivity, and any number of things deemed reasonable by the court. Depending on the trial some attorneys even have special assistants whose expertise is helping to select a jury.

Lawyers can learn a lot during *voir dire* by simply asking potential jurors about place of employment, prior involvement in lawsuits, and past criminal record. Body language and even how jurors' dress can give hints into personalities. This *voir dire* process is not meant to pry into an individual's personal background or discredit a person but is a means of deciding who will be a proper juror, able to render a fair, impartial decision. It took Frank Haddad several "strikes" before he settled on a jury he was comfortable with. One of the questions Steve Pitt didn't have to worry about and neither did Haddad was the death penalty. The government had taken that off the table in its previous trials and would do so here.

On Monday, June 21, 1976, a jury was impaneled around noon. Federal District Court Judge Rhodes Bratcher gave jurors a heads-up that this trial could last as long as ten days or two weeks.

Assistant U. S. Attorney Steve Pitt was introduced as the attorney for the prosecution, while attorneys for the defense representing Jim Simon were Frank Haddad of Louisville and Paul Lewis of Elizabethtown.

There was somewhat of a question from the court as to who was sitting next to Pitt at the prosecution table. It was ATF Agent Bill Rockliff, not exactly an attorney, but one who knew as much about the case as anyone. Pitt was sure his team and the investigators of federal and state lawmen had enough evidence to connect Jim Simon to the murder.

The government's key witness was David Cooper Walker.

Walker testified about his meeting in Cave City at Jerry's Restaurant with Johnson and Simon in the first part of December 1974. He told of a warm friendship he had developed with Johnson. He said he felt remorse over the death of Mrs. Rhodes, but that he would not have felt remorse over the death of Paul Rhodes because of some of the things he's done.

Walker said that it was Johnson who first contacted him, but both Simon and Johnson hired him to kill Rhodes.

Simon's attorney Haddad attacked the credibility of Walker's testimony in cross-examination, claiming that it was Johnson alone who had hired Walker and that Walker was now only testifying to keep his end of a bargain he had struck with federal authorities to get his sentence reduced.

Walker, who had been convicted of perjury previously, said he would not make the same mistake twice because it would only add more time to his prison sentence.

It was then that David Walker said something that many in the courtroom had not heard before.

He said the only reason he testified was because Simon and Johnson failed to give him enough money to keep the man who was first arrested for the bombing from talking. If they had come up with the money to keep Steve Monroe quiet after his arrest, he "would not be here today," Walker said.

Walker told that Monroe and Lloyd were to split $5,000 (However, Lloyd told me in a prison interview in 2018 that he and Monroe were to get $5,000 each).

Walker said he thought using the bomb was a "damn fool thing," but Monroe testified the same day that Walker knew all along that he planned to kill Rhodes with a bomb.

Walker told the judge and jury that he first found out that the bomb had exploded when he visited the Ford dealership soon after. He said Johnson was busy when he got there, but Simon took him aside and explained that it was Peggy Rhodes who had been killed and not Dusty. When Johnson came into the room, Walker said Johnson was quite upset and demanded that Walker get someone up to the Rhodes' farm to shoot Dusty. Walker said no.

Under cross-examination Walker told Haddad he did it because he likes new cars and money. He added that Mr. Johnson had become his friend.

Walker said he did not receive any of the money promised him. He said he paid Monroe $500 from his own pocket. He went on to testify that Simon and Johnson would have had to borrow the $10,000 to pay him.

ATF Agent Rockliff testified that on the car ride to Louisville after Simon's arrest, Simon questioned if Johnson could have set him up. Then he told Rockliff he did remember the trip with Johnson to meet Walker. He went along only to appraise a car.

When it was Rhodes' turn to testify, he said he believed Simon tried to kill him for the money that the Ford dealership would have received from the insurance policies on his life that listed the dealership as beneficiary.

Paul Lewis, an Elizabethtown attorney, had been hired by the Simon family to work with Haddad in defending Jim Simon. At fifty-three years old, he showed a tough exterior that matched his reputation of being one of the best lawyers in Central Kentucky.

Rhodes described to Paul Lewis that he and Simon had been good friends during their time of working together. Lewis went on to describe to the jury their relationship as Rhodes taking Simon in and teaching him the automobile business. He painted a picture of Simon being a good learner, soon becoming sales manager and buying stock in the business.

Testimony revealed that Rhodes, Simon, and Johnson entered into an agreement that stated the corporation would maintain a life insurance policy on Rhodes' life for the amount owned to him with his wife, Peggy, being the beneficiary.

Rhodes offered that he had three life insurance policies assigned to Citizens Bank in Elizabethtown to secure a small business loan. He said the business loan was one that Simon and Johnson were assuming in the corporation.

He said his three life insurance policies were to be replaced by policies on the lives of Simon and Johnson and that the beneficiary on Rhodes' policies were to be changed to his wife but never happened.

Bookkeeper Alma Williams testified that she had worked for Simon-Johnson Ford for one year and that Simon had asked her to check with the headquarters of Home Insurance Company to determine how much life insurance their company had on Rhodes. She said she wrote down the information on a slip of paper that Jim Johnson quickly took from her. When asked during testimony, she thought the request from Simon was unusual.

Bobby Johnson, Jim Johnson's son, took the stand in testifying against Simon and said his father thought Rhodes had made misrepresentations about the company when his dad bought in. He said that Simon and his dad had met with Attorney James Scudder in late 1974 and early 1975 to discuss suing Rhodes.

The younger Johnson also told the court that Simon had refused to visit his dad in Hardin Memorial Hospital in April 1975, while his dad was recovering from a suicide attempt. Bobby Johnson said he spoke with Simon over the phone and that Simon told him it would not look good if he visited Bobby's dad.

Later Bobby Johnson testified he never heard his father make any threats on the life of Rhodes.

Jim Simon's wife was called to the stand. She said nothing of the bombing plans and that she was the one who handled the family checking and would have known if her husband had paid a killer.

U. S. Assistant Attorney Steve Pitt asked Mrs. Simon about two checks that were written on December 16, 1974, on the company account for $250 each. One check was written by Simon and one by Jim Johnson.

It was the government's belief that the two checks were cashed by Simon and Johnson and that the cash was given to David Walker to reimburse him for the $500 he had given to Steve Monroe as a down payment on the $5,000 he had promised him for killing Dusty Rhodes.

Simon's wife said her husband bought her a microwave oven with the money as a Christmas present.

Jim Simon was able to produce a receipt showing that he had made a down payment of $100 for the microwave on December 18. He paid the remaining $315.75 on December 23.

In further testimony Simon said his relationship with Rhodes had always been good and that he never wanted him to leave the dealership. He said while they were together, Rhodes ran the business, and he managed the sales.

Simon said the reason he asked his bookkeeper to check on the amount of life insurance the company was paying was only an effort to look at cutting expenses. He said he was under pressure from Citizens Bank, Ford Motor Credit, and the Ford Motor Company to cut expenses.

James Payton said the dealership owed Citizens Bank approximately $250,000.

A representative of Ford Motor Credit said they lost around $200,000 when the dealership closed. He went on to say Simon and Johnson sold cars valued at approximately $100,000 without paying for them. In the automobile business there is a term "Selling Out of Trust." It is commonly used to refer to selling a car that has been paid for with a loan and then not using the sale proceeds to pay back the lender, in this case Ford Motor Credit. The lender cannot seize the car since it has already been sold to a third party.

On top of that Dusty Rhodes was still owed $108,000.

Adding up the numbers, if Jim Johnson and Jim Simon did in fact pull off the intended murder and collected the $150,000, it would have only been a temporary fix to a business that was spiraling downhill fast.

Simon, however, took the stand to deny any conversation at the Cave City Jerry's Restaurant about killing Dusty Rhodes. He said he did look at a car there to appraise. He denied drawing any kind of map for Walker to get to the Rhodes' farm, and he said he had never met with Johnson and Walker at the Ramada Inn in Bowling Green. And those phone records of calls to Walker? He said he never made any of them.

CHAPTER TWENTY-THREE

David Walker was an easy mark for attorney Frank Haddad when it came to credibility. As in many trials, especially murders, past records of defendants and witnesses are sometimes off-limits. For Jim Simon his life had been for the most part one of truthfulness. His defense presented a host of character witnesses who included a priest, attorney, banker, realtor, a couple of car salesmen, and a nurse.

Walker told the court he did not have a lawyer and that he had to file his motion for a reduced sentence himself. He added that federal attorneys had not given him any assistance whatsoever. He also said he had been denied the medical care he needs.

Being from a family of means, Walker's mother Irene could well afford to pay for lawyers and had done so several times in the past. However, there were government agents and state police who told how Irene Walker met with them to see how serious the trouble her son was now in.

The government felt like they had laid out a strong case against Simon. Producing phone records in December 1974 and January 1975 from the Ford dealership in Elizabethtown to Walker's unlisted phone in Bowling Green, the government didn't believe that they dialed that number by accident.

The financial pressure on Simon-Johnson Ford didn't just happen overnight. Bookkeeper Alma Williams said, "There wasn't any money when I started working, and there wasn't any money when it closed."

Walker said he was the only one who ever discussed the murder with Johnson and Simon. He said it was Johnson who insisted on the contract on Rhodes' life and described Simon as a passive participant in the plot.

As David Walker's testimony drew to a close, Assistant U. S. Attorney Steve Pitt turned to Walker and asked him why he was talking now.

"I'm in jail," he said. "(Carlos) Lloyd is in jail. (Steve) Monroe is in jail. (Jim) Johnson has killed himself. And this man (Jim Simon) is as guilty as I am."

Simon went on to blame his lapse in memory pertaining to meeting David Walker in Cave City with Jim Johnson on the fact that Simon-Johnson Ford sold 1,500 cars in 1974 and that he was in on 75 percent of the deals. Names and faces don't mean that much to me, he said. He did say that when he, Johnson, and Simon went outside after eating at the Cave City Jerry's Restaurant, he went over to Walker's car to appraise it while Johnson and Walker moved over to another area in the parking lot and talked. What they talked about, he didn't know.

Near the end of the trial during one of the deliberation breaks, ATF Agent Rockliff said Simon walked over to him and wanted to talk. To say the least the request was unusual. Here was the lead government investigator conversing with the defendant in a murder while the trial was still officially in progress. Rockliff said Simon told him that, no matter what the verdict was, he had no hard feelings.

"He told me he understood I was just doing my job," Rockliff said.

Rockliff continued. "Simon began to weep, saying, 'Goddamnit, I just didn't do it. If I'm guilty of anything, it's just for being so goddamn dumb.'"

ATF Agent Rockliff had been around Simon a lot, interviewing him many times, but he described Simon's words as chilling, with a sincerity in his voice. He added that the thought flashed in front of him that Simon might have been simply a victim of a complicated situation.

Haddad's closing argument was intense, if not emotional. As he had done throughout the trial, he attacked the government's most damaging witness against Simon—David Cooper Walker, a convicted perjurer.

Haddad said that it was Jim Johnson alone who had hired Walker and that Walker had brought Simon into the scheme hoping to get a reduced prison sentence.

Two witnesses testified they heard Johnson say that he was going to kill Rhodes, whom he thought swindled him in his purchase of the Ford dealership. Johnson had committed suicide four-and-a-half months after the death of Peggy Rhodes.

Haddad pointed out to the jury the government had failed to introduce any evidence or witnesses to support any of Walker's testimony. Again he urged the jury not to convict a person on the unreliable words of a convicted felon and a convicted perjurer.

For anyone who had followed the four-day trial, it had come down to believing David Walker or believing Jim Simon.

Frank Haddad, showing his skill, preparation, and ability to connect with the jury, closed by saying, "You cannot convict Simon on suspicion and conjecture. There was more than one reasonable doubt about his involvement in the bombing and that reasonable doubts must be resolved in favor of Jim Simon."

When the day started Judge Bratcher told the jury he thought they should get the case around 3:30 p.m., and the veteran judge almost nailed his prediction.

The jury deliberated for over two hours before returning to the courtroom to ask the judge for a clarification on the legal definition of conspiracy and his guidance in how they should determine if someone is guilty or not guilty under the conspiracy law.

The jurors returned to their deliberations after the explanation from Judge Bratcher, and ten minutes later, they were back in the courtroom with their decision at 6:25 p.m.

Not guilty!

Not guilty of two counts of charges that Simon was a member of a conspiracy to kill Paul F. "Dusty" Rhodes and that he aided and abetted in the explosion that killed Rhode's wife Peggy.

Jim Simon and his family were elated. Tears, hugs, and kisses were everywhere. It had been a difficult four months.

In many countries throughout the world justice comes from the top down—kings, monarchs, presidents, dictators or parliaments—but in America, justice is implemented from the bottom up. It's the people, ordinary people, who make up a twelve-person jury, which is the cornerstone of the judicial system.

A jury decides from the evidence and the laws whether the defendant is guilty or not guilty. The words *innocent* or *not innocent* are not part of the vernacular. Clearly, however, the defendant is presumed innocent and may not be found guilty unless the prosecution meets its burden of proving to the jury that the defendant is guilty beyond a reasonable doubt. If the prosecution fails to meet its burden, the jury must find the defendant not guilty.

Reasonable doubt does not mean any doubt, but it does mean substantial doubt. That's what Haddad was seeking. After the jury heard all the evidence, Haddad wanted them to actually doubt his client was guilty.

With presented evidence from both the prosecutor Pitt and the defense Haddad, the jury could be convinced Simon was guilty, and minutes later conflicting evidence presented could cause them to now have reasonable doubt.

Rockliff recalled that before Simon's trial, Steve Pitt had said to him, "Rocky, I really think we have enough evidence to convict. I think he had a motive and something to gain."

Years later Rockliff said he was doubtful about Simon's indictment. "I just think he was dumb about what was going on."

Post Simon trial Assistant U. S. Attorney Steve Pitt had his thoughts.

"In the court of law, Simon was not guilty, but in the court of public opinion, Simon was guilty," he said.

For the twenty-eight-year-old Pitt, the trial was nerve-racking. He had met with informants during the scary times of prosecuting bank robbers, gambling rings, and tax evaders in the more than thirty jury trials he tried, but this one was different.

"The Peggy Rhodes trial was the most intense," he said.

Steve Pitt grew up in Lewisburg, Kentucky, a small community in Logan County. He knew Jim Johnson and his history as a respected lawman. He also knew Jim Simon's brother from their days as students at Western Kentucky University.

Even though Pitt lost the Simon portion of the Peggy Rhodes trial, he and Bob Bridgewater received an ATF award for their efforts in the case.

Those close to the case on both sides had their opinions, but their opinions didn't matter. The only opinion that mattered was the jury's.

Remember, it was Simon's attorney, Frank Haddad, who said a person is never guilty until the jury says he is guilty.

ATF Agent Bill Rockliff said Jim Simon went to trial not guilty, and when it was over, he was still not guilty.

At the conclusion Judge Bratcher ordered a refund of $2,000 to James Corbett for the bond money he had put up for his stepson's bond.

"Jim was never the same person after the murder and trial," said one of Simon's best friends. "In E-town it was talked about … yet it wasn't talked about, depending in what group you were around."

"Even though Jim never went into any depth in conversation about the murder, he left an impression he might have known something was up as it related to Jim Johnson. But Jim [Simon] always told me he was innocent."

Later Jim Simon picked back up with his real estate after the Ford dealership changed hands, and he dabbled in selling some used cars, something he had been very good at.

"When he died he sat down to read the Sunday newspaper at his house and died," said his good friend.

It was December 23, 2001. He was sixty-years years old.

CHAPTER TWENTY-FOUR

B ut all the story hasn't been told pertaining to some of the central characters that were involved in the murder of Peggy Rhodes on Youngers Creek Road.

David Walker dodged a bullet when it came to a prison sentence in the murder of Peggy Rhodes. He served seven years of a ten-year sentence in Leavenworth Federal Penitentiary, with the last year being in Memphis. After his release, the adopted son of wealthy parents in Bowling Green, Kentucky, still had the opportunity to make his life right for his wife and three children.

He told several people he was going to make a difference in people's lives, especially the poor.

In 1985, at the age of fifty-eight, David Walker opened Walker Memorial Mission, a church-operated homeless shelter in Bowling Green. He may have had the best intentions in the beginning, but all of that changed when Walker, in an effort to raise money for his shelter, implemented bingo as the catalyst. As only he could do, soon millions of dollars were finding their way into Walker and his partner David Dennison's pockets. It was so successful in Bowling Green that Dennison opened a branch operation in Owensboro, Kentucky, sixty-five miles to the west.

To be legitimate Walker had to acquire his bingo cards from the state. It just so happened that the cards were officially registered and in a numbered sequence, leaving a trail of cards sold by Walker and Dennison. The state, knowing what each bingo card sold for, gave local authorities the exact amount of money Walker and Dennison's bingo games brought in. The cards sold did not match with Walker's church deposits. The checks were recorded but not the cash. And for anyone who has ever played "pay-to-play" bingo, rarely are cards purchased with a check.

While $35,000 was deposited in Walker Memorial Mission's account, the belief was that several million dollars' worth of cards had been sold over the last three years. In 1977, a young Bowling Green rookie policeman named Bruce Wilkerson had come on board. With eyes wide open he set out to do what he was hired to do: keep law and order.

"We were told as rookies who to be on the lookout for … people that always seemed to be in trouble, and David Walker was one of them," Wilkerson said years later. "When his church operation began, it might have been legit, but it didn't take long for us to start looking at it as more of a gambling operation."

But by then things had become complicated. Walker had created a relationship with the Rev. John Frederick of the Apostolic Lighthouse Church in Bowling Green to use the church's tax-exempt status. It surprised few when the proceeds of those bingo cards began to disappear.

Rev. Frederick went public, telling the media $6 million meant for the homeless shelter was missing. He said $9 million had been brought in, and maybe $3 million had actually gone to Walker Memorial Mission.

"Maybe somebody can find out where it went, but it didn't go to feed the poor," Rev. Frederick said in a deposition in Warren County Circuit Court in a divorce case involving Walker's ex-wife. The couple divorced in 1987, two years after Walker started his bingo-church operation.

Newspapers across the state had latched onto the "bingo-church" story.

Frederick gave Walker's estranged wife and her attorney records of the shelter's operation, which were to be used as part of Walker's property settlement.

Frederick, who operated concessions at the bingo games, said about 88,000 people attended bingo between 1985 through 1988, and each would have averaged $50 per night. Walker and Dennison also had a pull-tab game similar to a lottery ticket that would have raised a similar amount as bingo, he said.

Book records showed that checks, but not cash, from the bingo games were deposited.

Walker's Memorial Mission, operated by David Dennison in Owensboro, was raided by police and four special IRS agents in November

1988. Records of the two years there showed Apostolic Lighthouse received about $11,000, Frederick said.

Lighthouse ended its affiliation with Walker in Bowling Green in August 1988, ending their tax-exempt status.

Three months later David Walker and David Dennison, who each had been driving new Lincoln Continentals and were referred to as Bingo 1 and Bingo 2, were arrested.

"The church thing and all the stuff David was doing with it came from a con (convict) he had done time with when he was in the Memphis Federal Correctional facility," his ex-wife said. "It was all scary. David couldn't carry a gun due to his being a convicted felon, so we drove two cars when we went certain places. I'd have the gun in my car."

It became a challenge to Wilkerson to keep an eye on Walker and eventually he was involved in shutting down the illegal church and gambling scheme.

Records showed Walker was arrested on two counts of promoting gambling and engaging in organized crime. But in March 1989, he managed to once again reach a plea agreement.

Ultimately he was charged with promoting gambling, engaging in organized crime, possession of a controlled substance, possession of gambling records, knowingly receiving stolen property and being a persistent felon offender.

The persistent felon charge was an understatement. After all, it hadn't been that long ago that he had been the catalyst in the murder-for-hire contract killing of Peggy Rhodes in Elizabethtown.

Walker's wife and three children had their bouts of living in fear because of their husband's and father's criminal activities and criminal friends.

"One day a known criminal who had done time in Atlanta (prison) showed up at my home, making threats to me," Walker's wife said. "He said he had friends who could either testify for David or against David. It was a shakedown, wanting money from us. I was scared. He was terrorizing us. I called ATF. It was so bad for us there was even talk about us going into the witness protection program."

Despite a list of crimes that would land most people not in jail but under it, Walker pleaded guilty but received no prison time.

Bruce Wilkerson, the cop who later became mayor of Bowling Green in 2011, recalled that, "No one locally wanted any part of this case, so it was worked out by the Commonwealth Attorney's office that instead of receiving jail time, Walker would leave the state of Kentucky for five years."

Wilkerson remembered, too, that Rev. John Frederick was later arrested on gambling charges.

With Walker now "sentenced" to staying away from Kentucky for five years, it still didn't stop the proceedings for the divorce settlement with his ex-wife.

On August 19, 1989, the sixty-four-acres known as Walkerhurst Farms, including the 2,800 square foot stone house, went on the auction block. Considered one of the prime properties in all of Warren County, Thomas R. Hunt Auction & Realty had been selected to preside over the court-ordered sale.

Walker's parents, Edgar and Irene, bought the property from Mayme Frances on September 4, 1948, for $36,667, considered a lot of money for the time. Located on what was then Cemetery Pike on the outskirts of town, it was a perfect spot for the Walkers to build their showplace home, which they did in 1949. Built of stone, with four large columns in front, and a long tree-lined, 1,100-foot driveway leading to it, and sitting back off the road, it had the appearance of a southern plantation house.

Edgar Walker died in 1967, and Irene, for over fifteen years, let the house fall in disrepair before passing away in 1982.

The Walkers also owned a prime piece of real estate closer to downtown. It was where the old Fairgrounds were located and later, on a 100-year lease, it became what it is today, the Fairview Plaza Shopping Center on 31-W ByPass. It, and a carved-out area with a car wash, had been a legal, steady source of income for David Walker for years. But it, too, would be sold.

With David Walker exiled to who knows where, on the day of the Walkerhurst sale, several in attendance said he was there. His ex-wife was still living in a small house behind the main house, so it was apparent her life was about to change even more.

Court records, on the day of the sale, listed the trustee of the sale as Soul's Harbor Non-denominational Church of God.

Walker in a creative sort of way transferred all his holdings to the Soul's Harbor Church. And wouldn't you know it, somewhere along the way, he filled out a few applications and paperwork and officially became Reverend David Cooper Walker. He was also listed as the minister of Hunter Hill Baptist Church located in Warren County.

"David was not supposed to be in the state of Kentucky, so I met him at the I-65 rest area on the Kentucky-Tennessee line and gave him two checks totaling almost $500,000," a Bowling Green attorney said. "I was told that David had been in Louisiana and Arkansas. I even heard that he hid the money in an Arkansas bank, but before he could get it out, the FBI got it. Who knows?"

ATF Agent Bob Bridgewater later told another story.

"Walker and his partner, David Dennison, supposedly deposited some of their money in Mexico. Well, both of them flew down to get it. When they got there, not only was their money gone but so was the bank."

David's wife said, "David lived high on the hog while me and my three kids didn't have anything. He had big new cars, boats, motorcycles, and his half-interest in Fairview Shopping Center (his sister Polly had the other half). And then there was Walkerhurst and all the other property the Walkers owned. David never included me in anything. I was not in his world."

Still, with all that had gone down with David Walker, his wife said, "I never gave up on him."

Walker had been diagnosed in 2001 with heart issues and kidney failure. Still in February of 2002, he rode his motorcycle to the Daytona 500. According to his wife he rode some in the area with Charlie Napier (a successful actor from Scottsville, Kentucky, whose claim to fame was starring with Sylvester Stallone in the *Rambo* movies), and even a few of the Hells Angels whom he had met in prison at Leavenworth.

David Cooper Walker died six months later in August 2002. He was seventy-one.

His story, however, was not quite over.

Edgar and Irene Walker's headstone is one of the largest in Fairview Cemetery in Bowling Green, located in one of the roundabouts with enough space to accommodate several burials. On the monument is "WALKER" centered between Edgar on the left and Irene on the right. And in the middle is the date they were married. At the foot on Edgar's side is a bronze, ground-level plaque showing his military service, date of birth, and date of death. The Walkers erected the huge monument before Edgar's death, and in all probability, Irene found it more affordable to do the plaque than have the updated engraving. And after she died nothing was done there except to bury her. No dates of birth or death.

With the Walkers' money, who knows why after Irene's death, David Walker and his sister Polly decided not to do anymore monument updating. If anyone wanted to know anything about the Walkers' final resting place, they would have to go to the nearby Sexton House. Was anyone else buried in the Walkers' plot?

"Yes, there have been four burials there," when asked about the Walker monument. "The Reverend David C. Walker in 2002 and his son in 2006. The son was thirty-six years old," she said.

No names, no dates. Just the few who know they are there.

David Walker's ex-wife says she and her children never received any money from the millions Walker received legally or made illegally. She says a former attorney of hers failed to file the proper documents to protect her real estate interest.

Chapter Twenty-Five

S teve Monroe, early in life, seemed to have it all. A supportive mother and father who ran a respected business, they even gave their son an opportunity to run his own. With good looks, who some described as a fast talker, he just couldn't avoid the pull to the wrong side of the law. Fast cars and fast money were impossible for him to say no to.

He had been warned by police to be careful. Steve Monroe, they told him, was headed in the wrong direction. Married for the first time at nineteen, he couldn't grasp the responsibility that he had of being a husband and later a father. Instead he chose to join the corrupt climate that existed at the time in Bowling Green.

Stealing cars and blowing up things soon became his way of life. Teetering on expanding his lawless ways kept him out of "real trouble." His father, Beryl Monroe, ran a successful rent-all business in town and had enough money to keep his son out of jail when needed.

Those so-called minor scrapes with the law all changed when Steve Monroe chose to step up his criminal profile by dynamiting a Bowling Green business. He was out of control. His stealing cars had escalated to trying to kill people, and he was on a fast track to nowhere.

Monroe's "nowhere" turned out to be nine years in federal prison for murder. He had picked his poison, chosen like-minded friends, and destroyed his own life and the lives of his first wife and new son and then his second wife and daughter. He was only twenty-four.

In spite of having to repeat his freshman year of high school in 1968, there was nothing dumb about Monroe. He was well spoken and the letter he wrote to Assistant U. S. Attorney Steve Pitt after his murder conviction in 1976 proved he could write.

In that letter he begged Pitt not to send him to prison. Couldn't he just be let go? He would be good from now on. Obey the law. Go to college and even become a lawyer. Monroe had been so accustomed to getting out of trouble that even after making a bomb, setting it, and blowing an innocent woman to pieces, he still thought he could and would be set free.

"I will never, ever, ever become involved with anything against the law. I mean that more than anything I have ever said in my life Mr. Pitt. If for one moment I stray from this goal, I'll return to the penitentiary, no questions asked," he wrote to Steve Pitt.

At this point Steve Monroe had been in prison eleven months. He was re-sentenced to twenty years on July 29, 1976.

When he completed serving nine years of an original fifty-year sentence for killing Peggy Rhodes, he returned to Bowling Green on March 27, 1985. It didn't take him long to begin putting together a rap sheet that Al Capone would have been proud of. From April 9, 1990, to September 23, 1995, his police record showed nineteen entries. Though none showed any stolen cars or bombings, they did show lots of driving violations that included four DUIs. Not bad for someone who vowed he would return to the penitentiary if he ever broke any law again.

On July 18, 1996, Monroe got his wish. He was sentenced to three years in the Kentucky State Reformatory for being a persistent felon. He was moved around to several different state prisons before being released July 10, 1999.

Three years later Steve Monroe died on January 29, 2002, in Greenview Hospital in Bowling Green from what the death certificate described as sepsis and multi-organ failure syndrome. He was fifty-one.

Carlos Calvin Lloyd, unlike Steve Monroe, had a struggle from the beginning. With no guidance at home, lived life in a "every-man-for-himself" way, if any decision were made, right or wrong, it would be up to him. Unfortunately, most of them were wrong.

Lloyd has spent a good part of his seventy-three years in prisons around the country, and for someone whose life had been a disaster, he finally made a good decision. After prison stints in Terre Haute, Atlanta, and Talladega that totaled eight years, the federal prison system began an experimental program in 1983, and Lloyd wanted to be a part of it.

He was selected for the program and transferred to Butner, North Carolina, where he was permitted to wear his own clothes and even carry a little money. As he approached six months remaining in his sentence, he was even allowed to go to Bowling Green for Christmas.

Leading up to the experimental program, Lloyd had been a model prisoner, even earning his GED over a ten-month period, missing a perfect score by three points. For someone who had spent two years in the sixth grade and three more in the seventh, it finally looked like he had made some good choices.

He learned a skill as an IBM typewriter technician, and when he was released from prison after serving almost nine years, he was employed by a local office equipment company in Bowling Green.

At the time of the writing of this book, all but one of the principals involved in Peggy Rhodes' murder are dead. Carlos Lloyd is still living. And he is back in prison but not for killing Peggy Rhodes. He did his time for that crime. But like so many who finally get out, they do something that puts them back in.

Carlos Lloyd is serving a twenty-three-year sentence for sexual abuse of a family member. The crime occurred in 1992, but he was not convicted until 2001 and began his sentence in June of the same year. He is scheduled for release in 2024 from Kentucky State Reformatory in LaGrange, Kentucky. He will be seventy-eight.

EPILOGUE

Steve Pitt, the Assistant U. S. Attorney and the lead government prosecutor in the Peggy Rhodes murder trial, received an ATF Award in 1976
for his handling of the case. Presented by the Department of Treasury in
1977, the award proved to be a steppingstone to a position in the U. S.
Department of Justice's Public Integrity Section in Washington, D.C. At
the time, it was a new division within the DOJ charged with investigating and prosecuting corruption cases involving public officials.

For thirty-eight years Pitt was an attorney with the Louisville law firm
of Wyatt, Tarrant & Combs before becoming Kentucky Governor Matt
Bevins' first appointment as his General Counsel in 2016. In 2019 he
became the counsel and special advisor to the Attorney General's Office
of Kentucky, Daniel Cameron.

Bob Bridgewater, who went by "Bobby" to most of his colleagues
and friends during his early days in law enforcement, always knew
what he wanted to do in life and how to get there.

As a schoolteacher in Scottsburg, Indiana, in 1962, the one-time
high school basketball player was good enough to have been offered
a chance to play college basketball for legendary coach E.A. Diddle at
Western Kentucky University.

He set his sights on becoming a Secret Service Agent and even
passed the exam. However, he joined the Bureau of Alcohol, Tobacco
and Firearms of the U.S. Treasury Department.

For almost twenty years he spent time tracking down moonshin-
ers in the hills of Kentucky and Virginia; guarding several presidents,
beginning with Lyndon Johnson; and investigating bombings and
explosions.

In 1983, Bridgewater left ATF due to the mandatory retirement age of fifty-five for federal law enforcement agents.

Bob's daughter, Susie Mitchell, knew as a young girl that her dad's job was dangerous.

"He told me to always go with a crowd and not by myself ... to always notice who was around me," she said. "I know he had several contracts on his life because of all the people he had arrested."

For several years Bridgewater operated an investigative service that worked with insurance companies, corporations, and law firms. Then at the age of sixty-one, he was tapped to serve as enforcement director for the Kentucky Alcoholic Beverage Control Department.

When he retired he left a legacy of memberships in the Fraternal Order of Police; International Association of Bomb Technicians and Investigators; The National Association of Treasury Agents; and the Bureau of Alcohol, Tobacco and Firearms Association of Retirees.

Bob Bridgewater spent countless hours with me in reconstructing accurate timelines of the Peggy Rhodes murder. His immediate response to the bombing in Bowling Green of the mobile home sales office, several months before, was vital in solving the Peggy Rhodes' murder.

Of course there were others, and the unintentional omission of their names does not diminish their importance.

Here are some of those agents in the Louisville and Bowling Green ATF offices: Bill Haverstick, Dennis Price, Bill Rockliff, Andy Potts, Tom Quinn, Frank Guernsey, Jimmy Canter, Terry Hurley, Charlie Hill, Dick Johnston, Jack McLaughlin, Mike Springer, and Jesse Triplett.

If Ron Kapfhammer didn't win an award from the Kentucky Press Association for his coverage of the murder on Youngers Creek Road, he should have.

For days back in 1975 and into 1976, his coverage was front page, sometimes above the masthead of the *Elizabethtown News-Enterprise*.

His skills as a writer gave his readers an insight to the death of Peggy Rhodes, the investigation, arrests, and ultimately the trials.

Ron's thorough reporting even landed him a subpoena to testify in the trial. Because of his accuracy that mirrored the trial transcripts, *Murder on Youngers Creek Road* is a better book.

Ruth Howard Hudson, Peggy Rhodes' daughter, has been invaluable for her memories of that dreadful night in January 1975. Her emotions and those of her daughters Lara and Susan (son Mike was away in the Air Force) came rushing out in painting a picture of words about what Peggy Rhodes meant to them as a mother and grandmother. Although her death happened so long ago, to them it seems like only yesterday.

—ᵚ—

On November 31, 1979, dynamite was still an issue in Bowling Green. Though the criminal element in the city had diminished and bombings of businesses and individuals were no longer making news, ATF Agent Bob Bridgewater found himself working one more case.

Several tips about explosives being hidden somewhere in the city had come in to local law enforcement. Bowling Green City Policeman James Rogers said the only clue was it was located on a dead-end street near downtown.

An all-out search for the explosives was immediately implemented. Finally, city police were able to zero in on the exact location. It wasn't just a few sticks either. Five hundred pounds of dynamite were found and kept under heavy surveillance until an explosive team from Ft. Knox arrived in Bowling Green and destroyed it.

—ᵚ—

After Peggy's death, Ruth and her two girls moved to the farm on Youngers Creek Road to be with Dusty. Six months later they all decided to move to Elizabethtown. The convenience of being closer to school for Lara and Susan and work for Ruth played a big part in their decision. They rented a house on Sunrise Lane.

Dusty puttered around with his farm and cattle for a while, making the eight-mile trip from E-town to Youngers Creek Road on a regular basis.

In 1978, Ruth and the girls moved to Atlanta, and Dusty decided to move back to Louisville. He bought a used-car business on Preston Highway and a condo in the Popular Level Road area.

Years later, when his health began to fail, he moved into the Masonic Home in Shelbyville, thirty-two miles from Louisville. There he resided until his death in 1997 at the age of eighty-seven.

Paul "Dusty" Rhodes was buried next to his wife, Peggy, in the Colesburg Cemetery in Colesburg, Kentucky, only a few miles from their dream home on Youngers Creek Road.

—⁓⁓—

Years later Peggy's granddaughter, Lara wrote, "I remember being thankful for Jerry's (Gilchrist) presence. I think God put him in that place at that time, because he was strong enough to handle what he saw, and to prevent us experiencing an even more severe trauma by seeing Ga-Ga, their horse, and the barn as he did. I will never know what indelible marks that night left on him, because he passed away many years ago, without my being able to speak with him about his memories. But, I will always be grateful to him that he was there for us that night."

—⁓⁓—

David Walker's parents, Edgar and Irene, were close friends of my grandparents, so close that Irene and son David on occasion would spend the night at their house in Smiths Grove, Kentucky, fourteen miles from Bowling Green.

An old family diary of my aunt's documenting the years 1936–1940 detailed my family's association with the Walkers. One entry, among a multitude involving the Walkers, read, "Mr. and Mrs. E.A. Walker and David Cooper were at our house for Thanksgiving dinner and I went home with them to spend the night." The year was 1937, and David Walker would have been eight. Another one read, "I rode with Mrs. Walker to visit a military school in Columbia, Tennessee." That's the school David Walker attended for a short time.

Edgar and Irene were frequent dinner and supper guests at my grandparents' home. And, equally, my mother and aunt visited the Walker home, while attending college in Bowling Green, often spending the night. The well-worn diary, with the dry-rotted latch, was very revealing as to the closeness of the Walkers and my grandparents, aunt and mother.

There was even a time in the late 1940s that my mother would drop me off to stay for a couple of hours at Irene Walker's house on Sumpter Avenue, while she shopped in Bowling Green.

—◊—

As tragic as it was and seemingly with such low value placed on a human life, the only money that admittedly changed hands was the $500 David Walker gave Steve Monroe as a down payment on $5,000 to kill Dusty Rhodes.

It was a far-cry from the agreed-upon $10,000 and a new Ford Thunderbird that Walker said he was to get from Jim Johnson and Jim Simon.

To further add to the lack of complete closure in the death of Peggy Rhodes, consider that Jim Johnson in all probability was going to be indicted as a co-conspirator. However, when he died, so did any forthcoming criminal charges. In the United States a person who is dead cannot be charged with a crime. The case is dismissed once the court is advised that the defendant is deceased.

With Johnson dead, Jim Simon was left to stand trial. He stood before a jury of twelve men and women, and when the trial ended, he was found not guilty.

With Johnson dead and Simon found not guilty, the death of Peggy Rhodes seems, after all these years, still in search of something.

APPENDIX
Bombing Timeline in Bowling Green

October 15, 1960	Geo Dillard car City Councilman/liquor sales
October 15,1960	Siddens Music Company
January 23, 1961	Caribbean Club, 519 E. 2nd Street, 4 a.m.
Feb. 15, 1961	Cline's First and Last Chance Liquor
	29 sticks unexploded, Boatlanding Road
April 28, 1961	31-W Lunchroom
May 27, 1961	Horse Shoe Beer Depot
July 27, 1961	Wm. Gilchrist, 6 sticks @ Moose Lodge
Aug. 4, 1961	Toby's Place
Aug. 7, 1961	Calvin Starks car,
	part-time worker @ 31-W Lunchroom
Aug. 29,1963	Police Chief Wayne Constant,
	Car did not explode
Aug. 7, 1964	Det. Harry Ashby, car did not explode
Sept. 3, 1964	McClellen Stone Company,
	Smiths Grove, Park City — two bombs
Sept. 30, 1964	Wayne Constant lake cabin — fire
Oct. 22, 1967	Cardinal Billards
Oct. 2, 1968	Cutler Hammer Plant, strike related
Sept. 26, 1969	WLTV-tower
June 5, 1970	The Pub
Feb. 16, 1972	Police Det. Darrell Moody, home
Apr. 2, 1973	Main Office Lounge — 1st bomb
June 22, 1973	Main Office Lounge — 2nd bomb
Aug. 27, 1973	WKU Parking Structure, bomb found
May 23, 1974	Park City Mobile Home Sales
Jan. 13, 1975	Peggy Rhodes — death! Elizabethtown

ABOUT THE AUTHOR

Gary P. West has simple criteria when it comes to writing books. "I only take on a project that I will enjoy writing about and I only write about something I think people will enjoy reading," he says.

West grew up in Elizabethtown, Kentucky and attended Western Kentucky University before graduating from the University of Kentucky in 1967 with a journalism degree. At U.K. he was a daily sports editor for the *Kentucky Kernel*.

Throughout his extensive career he has served as executive director of the Hilltopper Athletic Foundation at Western Kentucky University, provided color commentary for Wes Strader on the Hilltopper Basketball Network, and served as executive director of the Bowling Green Area Convention and Visitors Bureau. He retired from there in 2006 to devote more time to his writing.

He is a freelance writer for several magazines in addition to writing a syndicated newspaper travel column, *Out & About...Kentucky Style*, for several papers across the state. Gary is in demand as a speaker and for book signings throughout Kentucky. This is his seventeenth book.

Gary and his wife, Deborah, live in Bowling Green, Kentucky.

Set of 8 Bunnies &
Eggs Easter Cards
#902042   ©Susan Winget

Set of 8
2 each of 4 designs

Happy Easter

Easter is Here

Just for You

Happy Easter

Shop all Easter at
currentcatalog.com

Easter
is March
31st!

MKT209

PRSRT STD
U.S. POSTAGE
PAID
MILWAUKEE, WI
PERMIT NO. 4550

Scan to shop
our online
catalog!

CUSTOMER #:   169578635

PROMOTION CODE:

LINDA WALTON
1832 N OLD PETERSBURG RD
PRINCETON, IN 47670

S24P2A01

/ 776 / 79505

Where staying in touch is affordable and fun™

Current

NEW! Personalized Brown Furry Bunny Easter Basket #818953

NEW! Personalized Pink Furry Bunny Easter Basket #818952

Easter is March 31st!

currentcatalog.com

INDEX

207